FATHERING A DESTINY

Growing Spiritual Sons and Daughters

Bruce Lindley

"FATHERING A DESTINY – Growing Spiritual Sons and Daughters"
by Bruce Lindley

4th Edition 2020

Published by ARC International (Aust) Pty Ltd

This book or parts thereof may not be reproduced in any form, stored in a
retrieval system, or transmitted in any form by any means – electronic,
mechanical, photocopy, recording or otherwise – without prior written
permission of the publisher, except as provided by Australia copyright law.
All scripture quotations are from the New International Version 1984 of the
Bible unless specified.
The Holy Bible, New International Version.
Copyright © 2005 by Zondervan publishers. Used by permission.

Copyright © 2020 Bruce Lindley

ISBN: 978-0-9942402-7-9
Printed in Australia

Dedication

This book is dedicated to the spiritual fathers in my life –

Che` Ahn, who is the best example of an apostolic father I know. Thank you Che` for fathering me and building my life; C. Peter Wagner for having the courage to declare publically the beginning of this Apostolic Reformation and then personally challenging me to jump into it; Lou Engle, for believing in my call to Australia & coming for THE CALL Australia in October 2004 to stand with us for this nation; Mark Tubbs who has unlocked the five fold possibilities for my life and every believer and for wanting to be my mate.

And those who haven't known their influence but still fathered me informally-

Pastor Tommy Barnett who so kindly encouraged my fatherhood journey; Reverend Jack Frewen-Lord who loved me unconditionally and believed in my potential in the beginning; Vic Stolar for always being honest with me in my formative years, Noel Woodford for showing me what a good loving father was and for loving me as a son.

And to my spiritual mothers –

Cindy Jacobs, who loves me enough to keep prophesying destiny over me every time she see me; Patricia King who released the anointing for generations over me; Doreen Woodford for loving God, her family and my children as a great Nan; and my mother; June Lindley, my greatest supporter, who always believed in me and whom God used in remarkable ways to encourage me.
And to my precious Cheryl, the wife of my youth, my gift from God who is the most remarkable person and best mother I have ever met.

And to all the fathers and mothers in our amazing ARC Apostolic Community – You are my family. We get to do this new wineskin together! How much fun & fulfilling is this?

To my awesome children – Rebecca, Rachel, Susanna, Sarah, David and all my grandchildren thank you for loving Jesus so passionately!

To ALL my emerging spiritual sons and daughters now and to come – what an honour it is to be your father! Your generation awaits you. Go and father and mother them!

Lastly, to my Papa God - who is my best friend, saviour and the lover of my soul. Thank you for revealing your father's heart to me!

Acknowledgements

This book wouldn't have been possible without the support and help of Cheryl Lindley and her amazing heart and creative skill.

I especially like to thank the following people:-

Katherine and Tom Ruonala from New Day Ministries, for their practical support of this book.

Geoff Slade from Transform7 Ministries for holding me to my goal of writing this book;

Special thanks to Marilyn Mc Kenney from Church Arise Ministries for her editing help and practical suggestions;

Contents

Dedication	3
Acknowledgements	5
Contents	7
Foreword - Apostle Che Ahn	9
Introduction	11
1 - Fathering a Destiny, who me?	17
2 – Apostolic Alignment and the coming Apostolic Reformation	25
3 - Positioned for fathering	37
4 - How to Father a Destiny	49
5 - Fathering Destiny Attitudes	61
6 - Learning to Establish your destiny	73
7 – Avoiding the Destiny Stealers	83
8 - Fathering will save you from the Destiny Destroyers	91
9 - Growing your Father's heart to change this generation	101
Contact details	111

Foreword

Apostle Che`Ahn

Bruce Lindley has written a timely book that helps us to both perceive God's apostolic strategy of fatherhood and pursue it. He has paved a way for others to enter into their destinies by revealing practical insights about how to be positioned and established so that you may become a spiritual father to the spiritually fatherless. This book will help launch a generation into the end-time apostolic ministry that is needed for the end-time harvest.

A fundamental link that joins people to their destinies is unveiled through Bruce. God's heart is to see us fulfil our destinies and He has given us the strategy of fatherhood. If everyone had fathers who would live to see their spiritual children fulfil their God-given destinies, then we would see the leadership transformation that we are contending for in society. As God transforms individual lives, those individuals, in turn, transform society.

We are on the horizon of an apostolic reformation in society and God is raising up and releasing Christians to influence every sphere of society. In light of this reformation, God is calling spiritual fathers to mentor tomorrow's leaders. He is looking for those who will give their lives to see the next generation fulfil their God-given destinies. When they do, God will cause His plans to unfold in their lives. Even as Jesus lived to see many sons enter into glory

Fathering A Destiny

(Heb. 2:10), we must live to see others enter into God's glorious destiny of being conformed to the ministry and image of His Son (Rom. 8:28) beyond the four walls of the church. He is inviting us to rise up and disciple our future world changing governors, presidents, prime ministers, lawyers, CEOs, film producers, artists, musicians, as well as apostles, prophets, evangelists, pastors, and teachers – in and out of the marketplace. Bruce clearly presents God's invitation and plan to spiritually father the leaders who are destined to disciple whole nations and lead in revival.

Through the pages of this book you will be invited into the journey of spiritual fatherhood and become an integral part of the coming reformation.

Che' Ahn
Founder and Apostolic Leader of Harvest International Ministry (H.I.M.)
Senior Pastor, Harvest Rock Church, Pasadena CA USA

Introduction

An Apostolic Fathering Reformation

I am convinced that God is bringing a Fathering Reformation around the world at this time!

Up until this past decade most Christians have been unsure of the role of apostles in the body of Christ. Some still get hung up on the use of the title and miss the real issue that this apostolic reformation is all about intentionally fathering a generation of spiritual sons and daughters.

One of the new things that God is doing is that He is revealing to leaders worldwide that ministry is not about them! The focus is no longer on *their* ministry, but on growing the ministry of those who are coming after them – a generation of spiritual sons and daughters. We are seeing such exponential growth in these sons and daughters, that many now believe that it is quite reasonable to expect the transformation of secular cultures to Christianity in one generation.

For decades leaders have referred to this as mentoring or discipleship. However I submit that 'apostolic fathering' is a development from both. Mentoring requires those being mentored to "follow my example as I follow the example of Christ" (1 Corinthians 11:1). The emphasis is on the "follow me." With this Fathering Reformation, I believe that there are now three levels of mentoring – by those in front of us (we all need fathers); peer level support, accountability and encouragement (we can father our peers as it is not about age or title but function); and those younger than us in God (intentional fathering of spiritual sons and daughters). This new Fathering Reformation encompasses to a lesser extent the traditional concept of discipleship that is essential for every Christian. It is what every Christian must do whether they are called to be a father or not! It is the fulfilment of the Great Commission of Jesus in Matthew 28:19-20. It is the systematic transformation of a person's life from spiritual darkness to the light of Christ – 'a Christ disciplined one.' A person is a disciple of Christ when they are constantly growing to be like Him.

What distinguishes fathering from the traditional concept of mentoring and discipleship is that it is 'next generational.' It involves the fathering of each person's unique destiny by a person who has a father's heart. Fathering is done intentionally and systematically. It builds, encourages, equips and then releases son and daughters (you must release them!!) into their destiny to transform the lives of others and then reproduce themselves again and again in the generation following them!

Just as you can develop the spiritual gifts in your life (1 Corinthians 14:1), you can also 'earnestly desire' to grow as a spiritual father.

Significantly, fathering the next generation has nothing to do with your gender – it an expression of a function that takes place when you understand the fathering role in a family! If all believers are part of the Bride of Christ, then I propose that when we speak on

Introduction

the concept of fathering, both males and females who understand the father heart of God can function as an apostolic father.

Fathering does not come naturally for most people. Just because you help conceive a child, does not automatically make you a father! Fathering is all to do with function NOT conception!

The good news however is that it is possible to grow a father's heart.

David is a classic illustration of this point. For four years he refused to father his son Absalom, as Absalom undermined his rulership as king. How do I know that? There wasn't any intentional acts of fathering by David, only weak indifference (2 Samuel 14 - 15). He allowed himself to be subject to his circumstances by doing nothing! However later in his life, something had moved in David.

We see just how dramatic that change was in 1 Chronicles 22:5 *"David said, "My son Solomon is young and inexperienced, and the house to be built for the LORD should be of great magnificence and fame and splendour in the sight of all the nations. Therefore I will make preparations for it." So David made extensive preparations before his death."*

David had become a father in the true sense of the word! He made sure his son Solomon was going to be a successful king by intentionally fathering him!

I grew up fatherless. Sure I had a physical father but I knew I badly needed a spiritual father.

By 1997 even though I was pastoring a church and had a great wife and five wonderful children I was floundering. I was desperate.

Something wasn't right and I knew it! I noticed that the emerging Pentecostal pastors in Australia all had something in common – they had all been fathered by a wonderful spiritual father, Frank Houston. He understood apostolic fathering decades ago! He had the revelation of intentionally fathering a "generation of sons" years before this current Apostolic fathering reformation.

By the late 1990's, I had travelled to the USA two years in a row to attend Tommy Barnett's annual Pastors Conference in Phoenix, Arizona because I saw what a great spiritual father he was. I even wrote to him and asked him to mentor me. In his typically loving fatherly way he graciously declined explaining that to be truly fathered it involved weekly intentional input and accountability and he could not do that from the USA when I was in Australia. I knew he was right!

At the end of 1999, after looking for a spiritual father for over twelve months, God spoke to my heart. He said, **"Stop looking for a spiritual father and become one"**. That set me on a wonderful journey that is still going today!

I have realized that to become a father, I first had to learn how to be a spiritual son. I knew what Romans 8:14 - 15 told me, "...*those who are led by the Spirit of God are sons of God. For you did not receive a spirit that makes you a slave again to fear, but you received the Spirit of sonship.....*"

However I saw there was a difference between knowing about being a son (information) and becoming one (formation). Christ had to be formed in me before I could be led by the Spirit of God! Then I could begin to learn to be a spiritual father!

Benjamin Disraeli wrote, "The legacy of heroes is the memory of a great name and the inheritance of a great example." I am not so

Introduction

much interested in a great name, but I am passionate about the inheritance, the legacy, that you and I are called to grow in the lives of those we must intentionally father.

This book is about learning how to grow in that spirit of fathering and in the process releasing a generation of sons and daughters into their destiny!

This is the only legacy that I now desire in life. I pray that after reading this book, you too will seek to father the destiny of others!

Chapter 1

Fathering a Destiny, who me?

This revelation that you need to become a spiritual father is a very important one. Until you have that revelation you cannot begin to understand how the function of an apostolic father works. Like all change it begins with a desire. It must be a desire to grow up to a level of maturity that enables you to father others. However that desire must be accompanied by a significant understanding of your own personal destiny! Has God called you to this? If the answer is yes, then you need to begin to grow as an emerging father.

One of the best ways to do this is to start teaching others how to discover their destiny and how to position themselves to step into its fulfilment.

For a number of years in our church I have been teaching people how to do just that.

Soon after I had begun this journey I had a defining moment!

A lady in our church burst into my office after I had preached on destiny the previous Sunday! Passion filled her voice when she said "I have got to know God's destiny for my life. I've asked God to show me but I haven't got an answer yet! You have got to help me."

As I began to speak, I heard my loving Father God whisper "Tell her she is called to preach the gospel." As I did, tears immediately filled her eyes as she began to tell me that when she was nineteen years old (some twenty five years earlier) she believed exactly what I had said. She even began to preach in her local church until shortly afterward her husband ran off with another woman. She was so devastated that for years she had closed that God desire down. Now all these years later her true destiny was being resurrected in her life!

Why? Because our loving Father God chose an immature spiritual father to speak hope and affirmation into an emerging daughter of God. The results were amazing.

The most important realization every one of us must come to, is that YOU AND I WERE CREATED FOR A PURPOSE and our purpose always includes OTHERS. I truly believe that we only come into fulfilment of that purpose when we start to pour our lives into others. This is the true meaning of success. When we have a successor!

To be a true spiritual father, you must have spiritual sons.

God says in Psalm 139:16, *"All the days (days of your life) were written in the book before one of them came to be"!*

Life is all about living your purpose. It is called a destiny! There is no expiry date on that destiny! Not just any destiny - God has created you for a divine destiny!

Most people never realize the full potential of their destiny!

I am convinced that one of the reasons for this is the lack of fathering of our generation.

As a young pastor in Australia in the 1980's I had spiritual leaders but, they would not have articulated their role in my life as a father. They were great pastors, role models and men of faith! I wanted to be like them in some ways but not in others! What was missing? Their mentoring and role modelling was informal not intentional! They couldn't really articulate how to function in their relationships. They just did it. I never felt that I could talk to them about my need for a father. I mean really talk to them – as a secure son would talk to a loving father.

The best way to become a father is to be fathered! And that is our challenge as we live in a nation that historically, has had fathers who haven't been able to express affection and affirmation to their children!

That certainly was my experience. My dad was a good man but he was emotionally scarred by his World War II experience, and it was something that he could never talk about. Like most men of his generation he could not vocalize his love to his children! This was very typical for his post war generation.

As a result we now have a generation of fathers who have not been fathered and this is why we have something very important to do now!

The truth is that I would have still been a fatherless father had something not happened to me when I was eighteen years of age. I was radically saved in my second year of university of all places. God came into my life with such power that all I wanted to do was

to tell people about Jesus for the rest of my life! I was two thirds of the way through a business degree and I didn't know what to do! The day after giving my life to Christ I travelled to New Zealand for seven weeks for a back packers holiday. I had no one to teach me about this new faith. I didn't even have a proper bible to read – only a paperback New Testament. There was so much fire inside me. I would tell everyone I would meet how the love of Jesus had changed my life and that it would do the same for them.
Sometimes this had amazing results with dramatic answers to prayer. I was so naive and ignorant in my zeal, that I was dangerous. One day I was hiking with a small group of fellow back packers at Mount Cook to photograph a glacier. One of them was a famous National Geographic photographer and I discovered he was a Jew. 'Well Jesus was a Jew' I thought, 'so this man must be a follower of Jesus too!' I waited all day to be alone with him so I could tell him my great news that I was a believer in Jesus just like he was and how much Jesus had radically changed my life! I expected him to share my joy! He didn't of course. Despite that I couldn't work out why he wouldn't want Jesus too, after all Jesus was and still is the only source of true life fulfilment! I badly needed to be fathered!

I had entered my late teens with something to prove, especially to my father who seemed to doubt my ability to succeed. I was driven to prove him wrong by making a million dollars by the time I was thirty. That was my first priority - to prove my father wrong. Then Jesus broke into my life and all that seemed insignificant. My life was so rearranged that all I wanted to do was to live my destiny in God. God gave me a number of mentors in my young formative years, even though they wouldn't have called themselves spiritual fathers.

Why was that? That wasn't the revelation we had at that time. I was well discipled though by those men. I was often encouraged that the key to spiritual growth was twofold - hunger & teachability. These things are great character forming qualities. However they don't automatically result in you becoming a spiritual father!

I learned that God has created each one of us for a divine purpose. It is up to us to discover it and live it!

Jeremiah 29:11 says *"For I know the plans I have for you,"* declares the Lord, *"plans to prosper you and not to harm you, plans to give you hope and a future."*

The key to happiness is finding your God-given destiny and doing it!

Regardless of what the popular western culture preaches, 'success' is not wealth, fame, nor a lifelong love relationship with 'Ms/Mr Right.' No! It is finding God's destiny for your life and living it!

Did you know that there are three plans or destinies for your life?

The first plan is God's plan for your life- John 10:10b *"I have come that they may have life, and have it to the full."* This is why you were created! This is your destiny! What fulfilment. What enjoyment! Nothing compares to life when you are living in God's perfect will according to His God-given plan for you that was made for you before even this world was created (Psalm 139:13-16). However, this plan doesn't that mean you live in isolation from others. The rest of this book is dedicated to explaining how to live out your God given plan for the rest of your life and change a generation in the process.

The second plan is the devil's plan to harm and destroy your God given destiny. Just as God has a plan for you, so the devil has a plan too! I call it the 'SKD plan.' How can I be so sure? John 10:10 also says *"The thief comes only to steal and kill and destroy"* (SKD*)*. It may start in the name of a so-called party hard lifestyle but quickly deteriorates. This is why it is so sad when you meet someone who subsequently through abuse or poor self-image becomes intent on self destruction – through self hate, addiction, self harm and even suicide. It saddens me so much when I see Christians choose this way of living after experiencing the freedom of Christ! The truth is your destiny is still by your free will choice. I have lost count of the number of amazingly gifted and called men & women of God that has chosen this plan. As a result they have stepped out of their God destiny. The result is disastrous, leaving a trail of broken marriages, families and friendships in their wake.

The third plan is the plan most people have fallen for! It is called 'SELF!' I believe the number one sin in society today is the sin of self-centeredness. The reason why our society is deteriorating so much is because of selfishness! Society bombards us with the need to put self first! Psychologists even teach that you have to look after yourself first! There is even a whole industry of self-help and self-improvement programs and books to help you please yourself! Television ads brainwash us with the need to please ourselves now – you can even get instant twenty-four months interest free finance to do it. History has taught us repeatedly that society declines when the family unit falls apart!

If you only think about yourself, you are not going to care for others – not even your own spouse and family! However, the more we only care about the success of ourselves, the more our society deteriorates. If you only love yourself you will not care about the feelings of others. You won't care about possession of others; in fact you will even help yourself if you want what they have. You won't bother with the need to tell the truth. You won't value the lives of other people. That is why there is so much violence, murders & even abortions! Why is that? I believe the answer to that question is our self-centeredness! You were never created to be self-sufficient. Over and over again I see self-sufficient people ending up with what they desire – by themselves! Alone. You see, the problem with the Self Plan, is that it only results in loneliness and fatherlessness!

God has so much more for you! Why settle for third best?

There is a destiny for your life that is so amazing. You mightn't end up being a billionaire or famous or the president of a major corporation or prime minister of your country but you will experience the most loved, happiest, fullest, fulfilled life that was ever possible. It will be because you have discovered and lived your God-given destiny.

The best way to do this is to be spiritually fathered - intentional systematic relational fathering!

So you have a destiny decision to make. What is it going to be? Self help, self loathing or destiny fulfilment by Godly fathering? The truth is that your existing lifestyle will tell you by what plan you are already living! Make a decision that will bless you, those who love you and most importantly God. Choose His destiny for your life and change others lives too.

What are you waiting for? You can be fathered in your destiny and then choose to be one who fathers others NOW!

Chapter 2

Apostolic Alignment and the Apostolic Reformation

God's love is being poured out in unprecedented measure at this time. It is season of 'restoring our souls' as the love of the Father is begun to be understood by His sons and daughters. It truly is a time to experience the Father's embrace, where we are restored into Godly relationships.

Over the last twenty years, much has been taught on the need for revival of God's church and a Jesus reformation of society. We need more of God than ever before so that a Jesus revolution can break out in our culture. I have a sense that it may come in a way that we haven't expected before – in the form of apostolic reformation.

God is restoring something to the body of Christ that has been missing for too long.

The best definition of 'restoration' is to be "brought back to its original condition." Many use the term 'revival' or "reformation' to describe what we believe needs to happen. But what does it look like?

I believe it is in the form of an 'apostolic fathering reformation.' This is what this book is about.

It starts with us. After all we are the body of Christ individually linked together. So He starts His reformation in us!

It does involve change. It begins with the need for restoration in our souls. The good news is that God promises to restore us.

Psalm 23: 1-3 says *"The LORD is my shepherd, I shall not be in want. He makes me lie down in green pastures, He leads me beside quiet waters, He restores my soul."*

The Bible teaches us that our soul consists of our mind, emotions and will. Psalm 23:1 tells us that His goal is for us to *"NOT be in want"*. God does not desire us to live with a broken soul! God's restoration causes us never to be in want again. He desires that our life is fulfilling and satisfying so that you are whole and complete in every way.

How do we begin to do that?

First, we must return to God with all our heart. Joel 2:12-13 tells us that we must honestly transparently and completely turn away from our old ways of living. Joel says that we must be so determined that we will 'rend or tear our hearts' so we can 'return' to right standing with God. This is true repentance. It involves a change of heart! After repentance comes 'restoration.'

For many of us, this would mean allowing God to heal and restore pain from years of disappointments, incidents and pain in our past. The prophet Joel saw this when he said in Joel 2:25 (NKJV) that God *"will restore to you the years that the swarming locust has eaten...."*

God wants to restore us today! The truth is that even though we were subject to the negative influences of others and our choices growing up, when we started out we were still not whole. Why? The answer is simple. We all have a sin nature. So when we talk about restoring our soul, we must ask the question "Restored to what standard?"

The answer is powerful. We were not created in our image of wholeness but God's image. Genesis 1:27 says just that. *"God created man in His own image."* So our restoration may not look like anything we have previously known. This is a good thing!

The Hebrew word for 'restore' used in Psalm 23:3 is 'shuwb' and it means 'retrieve, return, restore or reverse.' Phil Mason, the leader of the New Earth Tribe in Byron Bay, teaches people how to pursue deeper meaning in life. He says "when we ask God to 'restore' our souls, *(our mind, emotions and will) are renewed day by day by God in order to be conformed to the image of Christ. As all of the English words that are 're' words, 'restore' speaks of bringing something back to its original intended condition. This was before the fall of mankind through sin and our sin nature."*

So our restoration is a new thing. It does not just involve being healed from hurts or pain from our past. It involves looking forward to the restoration of our heart until our minds are completely transformed and renewed (Romans 12:2). Kris Vallotton from Bethel Church in Redding teaches that God wants us to call the glory out of others. In other words, the ultimate goal of this restoration process is to restore the hearts of others through our restored father's heart! This is the basis of this new wineskin "fathering reformation."

It seems to me that God is outworking this today in a number of ways.

GOD'S FATHER'S HEART

God loves restoring lives from brokenness to wholeness. This is His "father's heart" toward us. There are two key scriptures that describe what God is doing in this fathering reformation. How something finishes is always significant. This is even more so when it is the Bible. It is the final word so to speak. So when one of the statements that finished the Old Testament was the bold declaration on fathering we need to take notice. Malachi 4:5-6 says - "See, I will send you the prophet Elijah before that great and dreadful day of the LORD comes. He will turn the hearts of the fathers to their children, and the hearts of the children to their fathers; or else I will come and strike the land with a curse."

Malachi was what we call a Minor Prophet in the Old Testament. But this prophetic statement in Malachi 4 is hardly minor. In fact it is still speaking today! There are some who would argue that this prophetic word was fulfilled by the coming of John the Baptist & how he would prepare the way for the coming of Jesus, the messiah. Luke 1:17 says "And he will go on before the Lord, in the spirit and power of Elijah, to turn the hearts of the fathers to their children and the disobedient to the wisdom of the righteous—to make ready a people prepared for the Lord."

But there is a second aspect to the fulfilment of this prophecy that is still being outworked in us today! God is speaking to a new generation of spiritual fathers throughout the world to begin to turn their hearts toward spiritual sons. The more this begins to happen the more sons will respond by turning their hearts toward spiritual fathers so they can be fathered in true sense of apostolic fathering.

John McElroy in "Passing on the Baton" rightly declares *"To become spiritual fathers and mothers, the focus needs to shift FROM our perspective TO God's."* In other words, we have to develop eyes that are no longer on our self and our ministry and begin to see people as God sees them. This is more than becoming self less! It means we need to begin to look at people through God's eyes – with eyes of love & eyes that see the potential of others.

To do this we have to move from what I call an orphan to a son! SADLY THERE ARE MANY CHRISTIANS TODAY THAT HAVE AN ORPHAN SPIRIT. While I will speak more in depth about this in later chapter, I do know from personal experience that we all have to have what I call a Romans 8:15 Sonship Revolution. Romans 8:15 says – *"For you did not receive a spirit that makes you a slave again to fear, but you received the Spirit of sonship. And by him we cry, "Abba, Father."*

To begin this fathering journey we must decide that we will turn away from an orphan spirit to a spirit of adoption. It is a process. It begins by recognizing that you have a needed to be free from the unwholeness of being insecure, fearful and even manipulative in your identity and relationships. The starting point of this process (and it is a process) is to realize how much God the father really does love & accept you! The bible calls this the restoration of our souls but it is outworks in us by us deciding to change your focus from you to others!

When we allow Him to restore us this way, we begin to move from insecurity, pain and heartache to health, security and strong emotions. He moves our minds from lack of trust to faith. We begin to trust – both Him & then others! He restores us from guarded hard hearts to soft heart of love, acceptance and forgiveness to Him and others. As we begin to turn our hearts to those around us we experience more and more of the love of God. In this process of restoration the more loveable we are others and more others love us! We begin to receive more love of the Father from God and from those sons and daughters around us.

Our ultimate restoration is complete when the heart of the Father is formed in us. However by then it is no longer about us. In fulfilment of Malachi 4:5-6 this indeed is a season of an outpouring of the love of the Father. God's father's heart is to restore us to our original divine purpose so that we can turn our Father's heart to others.

God is showing his Father's heart to us so we can grow His heart in us for others. This moves us from a new wine experience of the love of the Father TO US to a new wineskin of growing the heart of a father in us so God's love flows THROUGH US for the body of Christ! So we must be willing to be 'restored' into God's original intention for us individually AND for the renewal of the body of Christ. This is only way this father's heart reformation will last!

APOSTOLIC REFORMATION

Many have also been saying that this season of Apostolic 'reformation' needs a new wine understanding. I have a sense that this is best understood by realizing that the father's love is the new wine and the father's heart is the new wineskin!

To do this, in keeping with Jesus teaching in Mark1:22 we need a new wineskin.

Psalm 23 in The Message - V2 and 3- *"you find me quiet pools to drink from.*
True to your word, **you let me catch my breath and send me in the right direction.**"

Many in the body of Christ are hearing the Holy Spirit say there is a 'change in direction' of how we do church. When God brings about a new thing, many begin to hear, see and catch it and we begin to be sent in the *'right direction'* that is being restored. This change involves us not only being restored, but also being realigned into Godly relationships. Again, if we accept that the definition of restoration is to be brought back to its 'original intended condition' then most of us have not thought these ways before. As such, we need a 'paradigm shift' in our mindsets to understand what God is doing in this season of apostolic reformation.

To do this we also have to change the 'way' we do church and how it is being outworked in His kingdom. God's Word never changes but we need to change our thinking to apply it to our society. If we don't change, then we don't allow him to 'restore' us by sending us in the 'right direction' and we become the obstacle to what God is wanting to do in this season. This is what Jesus meant when he said in Mark 2:22 *"no one pours new wine into old wineskins."*

So there is a correlation between restoring our souls and new wineskins for us as individuals and God's original intention for the body of Christ too! When we rise up into this, significant changes occur in us and through us. There is a release of life and restoration wherever we go. One *of* the most significant results is that hungry young people are drawn to your fathering heart and want to become taught by you to step into their own destiny of reformation. This is happening more and more around the world today.

If we refuse to restore our souls, then as Mark 2:21 says, *"it is like trying to sew a patch of unshrunk cloth on an old garment."* If we do this the reformation of our culture will not happen.

How is the apostolic reformation and alignment contributing to this restoration?

APOSTOLIC ALIGNMENT

To enter into this new reformation we need 'apostolic alignment.' For the sake of this discussion, we need to use the term 'father' and 'apostle' interchangeably. The heart of God the Father is being released into a new generation of young emerging apostolic fathers.

The good news is that God tells us in Ephesians 2:19-20 that we are "...*members of God's household, <u>built on the foundation of the apostles and prophets</u>, with Christ Jesus himself as the chief cornerstone."*

This is the basis of the restoration of the function of the ministry of the five fold in the body of Christ today. Ephesians 4:11 reinforces the importance of this apostolic reformation.

Ephesians 4:12 declares that the fivefold ministry is *"for the equipping of the saints for the work of ministry, for the edifying of the body of Christ."*
The Greek translation of the word 'equipping' (kartartistmos) means to be repaired, mend, as a broken bone needs to be properly aligned to heal.

So 'apostolic alignment' is the spiritual principle of bringing us into godly alignment with the leadership, accountability, and blessing of apostolic fathers who are flowing in this 'right direction'.

God is creating a new wineskin of many apostolic networks around the world made up of ministries, churches, missionaries and pastors who come into apostolic alignment with each other. They are apostolic networks of apostolic people.

It has been my experience through our apostolic network, H.I.M., that 'apostolic alignment' leads to a whole new level of blessing and prosperity by God. In the same way He blesses sons and daughters through a mother and father of a natural family, in this new wineskin, God is sets us in families of like minded people who share the same DNA of apostolic reformation.

Some of these tremendous benefits include increased levels of
- Spiritual protection (Hebrews 13:17);
- Divine order and the favour of God (Ephesians 6:1-3)
- Greater spiritual authority (Luke 16:12)
- Anointing of God (Psalm 133:2)
- Blessing of God (Psalm 133:3)

Che` Ahn, in his teaching on *'Apostolic Alignment, Accountability and Spiritual Authority,'* shares that breakthrough and release came when he received the revelation of the need to be under spiritual authority. He believes that 'the only one who is safe to lead is the person free to submit. You can't be in true spiritual authority unless you are under authority. You can't lead unless you know how to follow.'

Shampa Rice, one of H.I.M.'s apostles from India, says that the *'fearful favour'* from God comes on us when we are apostolically aligned. "Something visibly shifted not just in the spirit realm but in our everyday life (when we joined H.I.M. apostolic network).

Both my husband and I noticed how unexpected favour from unexpected sources caught us quite off guard. We were amazed as well as afraid! Why afraid one might ask? Afraid because we prayed for favour like this for years and never saw it materialize and then here was favour staring us in the face and we quite did not know how to respond..."

Shampa is right! The breakthroughs begin to powerfully happen. It is common to have long term prayers answered and provision released. It has also been my own experience that everything lifts into a whole new level of God's fearful favour when we align ourselves with an apostolic network. Everything increases and grows. This includes increase in the number of people coming to Christ through our ministry, financial provision and the supernatural supply of buildings and even wealth transfer. More than that, people often testify that they have finally 'come home.' They finally fit where they belong.

In the Old Testament, the God of Israel was the God of Abraham, Isaac and Jacob not just the God of Abraham. There was an alignment to blessing through spiritual fathers. Jacob honoured the blessing of God through his father Isaac even though his brother Esau did not. Jacob understood how important it was to flow with the blessing of God over his natural and spiritual family. There is an apostolic family that God wants you aligned with in this season of apostolic alignment and restoration. When you find this family and align yourself with its apostolic father then the blessing will flow through the family of God to you and then through you to others.

Through the power of your personal restoration as a spiritual son or daughter, God is releasing you to enter in to apostolic alignment and become an essential part of the apostolic fathering reformation that He is releasing worldwide today.

This is the time to rise up in to your destiny and father a new generation of spiritual sons and daughters. This is the true blessing of restoration.

Chapter 3

Positioned for Fathering

Choosing God's destiny for your life is very important but it is only the first step. To live your destiny you have to do something! You can't just sit back and expect God to do it all. So if you want to fulfil your destiny in life you have to position yourself to be fathered in your destiny.

If you don't, it is like getting into an elevator in a department store and pushing the button for any floor and assuming because God is in control, somehow, some way, you will end up at the right place at the right time! However this is not how life works and this philosophy is not Christianity. It is fatalism!

Your God destiny will not just 'happen'! Similarly, you are not going to wake up one day and find you have become a spiritual father or mother.

Each of us must 'position ourselves for destiny and for fathering!'

What does this mean? A position is a 'way in which a person is placed or arranged.'

To experience your destiny you have to position yourself.

This is exactly the same truth for you to receive blessing, healing, prosperity, and any faith desire in your heart. You must position yourself for the fulfilment of your destiny as a son and a father!

Sometimes positioning yourself requires significant change on your part – especially in terms of whom you hang out with! As my friend Col Stringer says – *"You will never soar like an eagle if you hang out with the turkeys!"* The older you get, the harder it is to change. Remember, a rut is nothing more than a grave with both ends knocked out! However as it is for your destiny that you need to change, it doesn't matter how much it costs, just go ahead and do it! I have been doing that for the last few years – we call them our transition years! Why? We have decided to purposely walk toward our destiny which has resulted in major changes in our role in our church. All change is uncomfortable, but even after just a few months, we are seeing amazing results!

The big deception is that most people think this is the case all the time. However, I have learnt that most destiny decisions require only minor adjustments in our lives. It may be an attitude adjustment and/or a minor adjustment in your daily life schedule – may be you just need to get up thirty minutes earlier so you do pray and read the Word every day. You can do that! The truth is, it is only you who can make these adjustments. Not the people around you.

A great example of a person who was willing to adjust her attitude and lifestyle for her destiny is Esther. She is also a good example of someone who had been fathered!

Compared to most of us, Esther's obstacles were huge. Both her mother and father had died when she was little. Her older cousin Mordecai brought her up. He did more than that - he fathered her! We can see that by how mature she was in the midst of hardship! Having your parents die would be tough enough for any child, but it gets worse. When she was a teenager, the king was looking for a new queen and decided that he would help himself to many young girls. He had a 'try before you buy' philosophy. It was not democratic or fair. In fact the girls didn't have a choice. It was the equivalent of people trafficking today! Esther was taken against her will to the king's palace to be part of his harem. However because Esther sensed the hand of God on this major incident in her life and she had been taught well, she had a Godly attitude. Sometimes all hell breaks loose after we have made Godly decisions.

When it was Esther's turn with the king, *"she asked for nothing other than what she was told to ask for."* She positioned herself again. Esther won the favour of everyone who saw her and especially the king.

This was the case for us when we moved our family of six across the other side of the world in 1989 so that I could attend Fuller Seminary in Pasadena California for four years. Our youngest of four children was just three weeks old! We sold all that we had in Australia and moved our four little children to the USA. Up until that point, everything had came together powerfully. God even sent an Australian missionary to our home church who had just returned from Fuller and told us everything we needed to know. He even arranged for a friend to meet us at the LAX airport, as we knew no one in Los Angeles. But as soon as we arrived in the USA all hell broke loose. So much so, that our new pastor, Che` Ahn, asked us "Are you sure you are in God's will?" We had nowhere permanent to live for six months, having to move seven times. When we finally found a house, the expensive Southern Californian high rents quickly consumed all our savings.

In the midst of no family support, and no income, God led us to a new church family, where new relationships, spiritual mentors and fathers had a dramatic impact on our future. After a while, despite the hardships, God started to bless us. I became Lou Engle's prayer partner every Monday morning. We formed a covenant relationship with our pastors Che` and Sue Ahn that still exists today! Yes it was tough, but we were willing to be mentored in our lives, our marriage and the raising of our children. We needed them more than we realised at the time and today they have become our spiritual mum and dad!. My mentor Lou Engle and spiritual father Che` Ahn came into our lives and revolutionized our destiny fulfilment which is still being outworked today!

We are told in Esther 2:17-18 that the king was attracted to her more than any of the others and won his favour and approval. As a result she was made the queen! Isn't that a lovely story?

However Esther became queen because of God's favour - and she knew it! The blessing wasn't the end in itself! So many Christians get promoted, or blessed, or received an unexpected financial windfall and say, "Hasn't the Lord been good to us!" but they do nothing with that blessing.

God always blesses us for a purpose and that purpose is always bigger than you. It always involves God using you to build others.

We're told in Genesis 12:3 that Abraham was blessed to be a blessing. God said to Abraham, *"all the people of the earth will be blessed through you"* and we are blessed today because of father Abraham's obedience. Like Abraham, there has been a generation of fathers who have had no role models. As a result they often conceive acts of the flesh (Ishmaels) as he did. But if we are willing to submit ourselves to the wise advice of our fathers, we would be saved from so many false starts and mistakes that we regret later in life. Esther soon realised why she had become queen. She realised what her destiny was!

An evil noble called Haman was given the highest honour in the nation. Everyone had to bow before him when he walked past! However Esther's cousin Mordecai refused to bow down to anyone but God. So Haman devised a plot to destroy Mordecai and worse still, all of Mordecai's people too – the Jews. It was going to be genocide for the Jews!

What Mordecai did next was the act of a spiritual father! He told Esther the truth! Because Mordecai had fathered her growing up, he was able to appeal to Esther for help (Esther 4:8) and urged her to go into the king's presence and beg for mercy for her people. However there was a major problem. There was a death penalty against any person who approached the king without being summoned into the inner court. So if she did this, it was very likely she would be put to death just like the former queen. What follows was Esther's destiny rise up moment! Mordecai challenged Esther, saying, *"who knows but that you have come to your royal position for such a time as this"* (Verse 14). Again, Esther responded with a destiny fulfilment decision, *"I will go to the king even though it is against the law, and if I perish, I perish."*

When we come to that place of absolute obedience, we need maturity to make wise choices.

There will be a moment of truth for you when you position yourself to step into your destiny. Obstacles will always come right after that decision. You need to ask yourself 'how determined are you to step into your destiny and willing to listen to tough advice?'

Esther was prepared to do whatever was asked of her. So should we! Esther saw a supernatural and unexpected result. God intervened because Esther rose up into her destiny. Her decision resulted in her whole race being spared from genocide. Amazing favour followed. It was favour for a fulfilment of a divine purpose.

We must never lose sight of our divine purpose. We could never have imagined the divine connection God was making between ourselves and Che and Sue Ahn and Lou and Therese Engle.

Every step in God's divine purpose is NOT always obvious. But if we keep walking toward our destiny like Esther did, regardless of the obstacles, it will result in great blessing and position us for destiny fulfilment.

The Nehemiah Moment

The Jews were in exile in another land. Nehemiah, a Jew, was cupbearer to the foreign king when news came that the walls of Jerusalem had been broken down and the gates burnt. Nehemiah was moved by the news. It was not just an emotional reaction. It was his divine destiny moment – the Nehemiah Moment!

You have a Nehemiah Moment that you can enter into too. It is your destiny moment. What are you most passionate about? What was the God idea that you were passionate about when you were younger? What stills moves you today? If you had the opportunity and unlimited resources what would you do for God? The answers to all these questions are your God destiny. All you need to do is decide to do it!

Nehemiah asked the king *"Would you send me to Jerusalem so I can rebuild it?"* (Nehemiah 2:2-4). The result is he was given favour and the king sent Nehemiah back to Jerusalem to begin the work! Nehemiah rose up and stepped into his destiny and so must we.

You might think that because he was obeying God and his God-given destiny, then there would be no problems. It would be all smooth sailing and they all lived happily ever after! But that is not true. In fact, all hell broke loose and worse. Nehemiah 4 tells us that people rose up and ridiculed him. The ridicule progressed into anger (verse 7) and a plot was devised to fight against them and stop what God wanted them to do (verse 8).

Too often a lot of Christians who live by the 'open door' philosophy of life, which argues that if God is in something it, will happen without any obstacles. It also sees a 'closed door' as a being an obvious sign that this is not what God wants. That is not what the Bible says. Jesus said in Matthew 11:12 (KJV) that *"the kingdom of heaven suffers violence and the violent take it by force."* I teach my spiritual sons that sometimes we have to kick down the doors of opposition! That is what Nehemiah did. They rose up and they prayed (Nehemiah 2: 4-5) and worked hard (verse 6) and guarded the wall day and night. However verse10 tells us that they realised their strength was running out so they needed a strategy if their destiny was to become a reality. That's why YOU need a strategy.

We need to learn from Nehemiah's strategy. He did four main things.

1st Strategic Alignments

Nehemiah was very strategic in the alignments that he made. Bishop T.D. Jakes says we need to be wise in the relationships we form and ensure they specifically help establish our destiny. The wisest relationship you need to choose outside of your spouse is who your spiritual father should be! A spiritual father will always have the ability to reproduce spiritual sons and daughters. Look for the fruit before you choose. Then form a lifelong covenant that will only ever bear fruit. I used the word *covenant* purposely. Covenant is misused and misunderstood in church today. People stay as long as it is convenient then leave at the first difficult strain or tension. My wife Cheryl always says that God puts you in families for a reason - a lifelong commitment to an imperfect person. Why? So Christ may be formed in you!

Nehemiah did just that! Nehemiah 4:13 tells us they worked and prayed in family groups.

God sets us in families for a reason and that reason is destiny fulfilment. It is so important you get this. All of us have been put in two families by God - a spiritual family and a natural family. It is for a destiny reason. Don't go changing families. The only time it is right to change a family is when the Lord promotes you to have your own family. Even then, this apostolic fathering requires you to be apostolically aligned! There are many ministries that are beginning to understand this need. That is the reason why the Lord is raising up so many apostolic networks - so we can be positioned in families for ultimate effectiveness and relationship!

2nd **Refuse to fear**

One of the greatest obstacles to your destiny is fear. Typically fear is due to a lack of true insight into our circumstances. Not surprisingly fear is one of the key strongholds of evil. It is the real reason why people won't align themselves apostolically or choose not be fathered. The antidote is to believe the truth of God's Word.

God says in Isaiah 43:1-2 *"Fear not because God is with you."* Paul said to Timothy (and to us) in 2 Timothy 1:17 *"God has not given you the spirit of fear, but of power and love and a sound mind"* (KJV). But most importantly, *"God is love and there is no fear in love"* 1 John 4:18.

Don't fear to be bold with pursuing your destiny! The result will be just like it was for Nehemiah (Nehemiah 4:15) God will begin to frustrate the enemy's plans. But you need to be careful, sometimes it looks like you have breakthrough when you have only won the first round and the fight has just begun.

3rd Keep your guard up

Never be complacent. You are in a spiritual fight for your destiny. So many people think that when they become a Christian all their problems will cease. However you have just enrolled in a spiritual battle. John Wimber used to say that too often a Christian's attitudes were likened to someone arriving at a dock to get on a cruise ship only to find that it was painted grey and it was a battle ship. Why? You are at war. You are in a fight. This is why we need to pray in the Spirit and read the Word each day.

This is why we need to be apostolically aligned. Ecclesiastes 4:12 *"Though one may be overpowered, two can defend themselves. A cord of three strands is not quickly broken."*

This is how we keep our guard up!

Nehemiah 4:18 tells us that Nehemiah and his men were armed at all times. This must be our challenge too. I have experienced that after fasts, conferences and breakthroughs it is easy to let our guard down. We must keep our shield of faith up at all times.

4th Fight for your destiny

When we were in Che Ahn's church in Pasadena in the early 1990's, we were taught very well on how to train our children. One of the main principles we learnt was the need for our family to pray together every morning. Since our children were little, we have had family prayer times every week day morning with incredible benefits. Now that our children are young adults, we should not be surprised that they all have a passion to pray for a radical Jesus revolution in their generation. They do this with extraordinary actions such as being trained at Lou Engle's Justice House of Prayer and standing in prayer outside our state government legislature for hours with LIFE tape over their mouths. Why? Because they have learnt through example that prayer is one of the ways you fight for your destiny.

When you position yourself every morning you are ready to hear the voice of God and step into fight mode when needed. So if you need to fast and pray, then that is what you do.

If you keep the fight up, eventually the obstacles will be removed - just like Nehemiah 6:15-16 and you will no longer be intimidated. Instead, the spirit of victory opens up and your destiny begins to come to pass. This is how you position yourself for destiny.

Fathering a destiny involves applying these principles in our life before we can impart them to others. This is why fathering is a process of formation and not just an occasional action. We must allow Christ to be formed in our character. I have discovered that God allows you to begin this fathering process in others before you are perfect yourself!

Often it is in the intentional fathering of a son's destiny that causes us to be confronted with the need to grow more in that area. The intentional instruction highlights the development of the fathering process in us.

As well your father's heart begins to grow the more you intentionally father others. Fathering resources, examples, and scriptures seem to jump out at you. People begin to see and hear the father's heart in you. Those with a similar heart are divinely connected to you. Young sons and emerging fathers are drawn to you. Don't be surprised. You have been called to father destinies and you are a part of what the Holy Spirit is doing in this apostolic fathering reformation now.

Chapter 4

How to Father a Destiny

We planted a church on the Gold Coast called Set Free. It was a street level church. We had a very strong outreach to people who normally wouldn't darken the door of a church. We preached the gospel, fed the poor and reached out on the street each week. Each year our hip-hop dance team and I travelled to Indonesia for an outreach mission's trip. No I don't break dance but we preached often in schools, colleges, markets as well as churches after the team danced. We worked very hard over a ten day period sometimes travelling eight hours a day to perform and preach the gospel. We always had an amazing response and see hundreds of Muslim and Hindu youth come to Christ.

One evening, after a very long day, we were asked for an interview on one of the most popular radio stations in Denpasar. Even though we were exhausted and still getting over jet lag, three of us went to be interviewed. It soon became very obvious that they were only interested in talking to the two break-dancers, and not me. So after an hour sitting in the dark studio listening to an interview where every answer had to be translated into Indonesian, I started to fall asleep. Time and time again I would catch myself about to slide off the chair onto the lush thick carpet on the radio studio floor. Finally I couldn't keep awake any longer, so I decided to go over to a corner in the studio and lie down on the floor rationalizing that no one would notice me there. Within seconds I was asleep, snoring loudly! The problem was the interview was live to air and an audience of three million people had heard my snoring! I awoke with a start, realizing instantly what I had done. Apologetically I retook my seat feeling embarrassed.

Almost instantly I heard the Holy Spirit say "Son, a lot of people are sleeping through their destiny!" I knew I had heard from my heavenly Father. He was teaching me that most Christians don't know how to position themselves in it.

This is especially true in this season of apostolic fathering. This apostolic reformation is all about knowing which sphere or mountain you are called to transform in your life. There are now many who are teaching the seven mountains or spheres of influence teaching. C. Peter Wagner, my former professor at Fuller Seminary and great Apostolic Father, has taken this teaching a step further. In his book 'Dominion!' he teaches that we are not only called to a specific mountain but we must exercise dominion authority in the workplace where God has positioned us, so we can transform society. This is how we will fulfil The Great Commission. Not through the church converting people to them, but by releasing people into their sphere of influence and fathering them to the point where they transform their world. To do that we have to position ourselves so we grow in our ability to take dominion in our mountain.

So it is one thing to discover your destiny, it is then another to be positioned in it.

T.D. Jakes, in his tremendous book "Reposition Yourself", says that three things are needed to begin to be established in our destiny.

We need a revelation of our calling

Revelation of our destiny begins with a growing awareness of a desire to do a certain thing with our lives. Traditionally many have used that desire to explore career possibilities. Some have even discovered their life partner that way. Most importantly that desire must turn into a passion, which in turn will become THE vision for our future.

The best example of this is Steve Irwin, the now deceased Crocodile Hunter. In an interview before his premature death, he talked of his desire as a young man to work with wildlife and how it turned into a burning passion to rescue wild life. In an interview with Andrew Denton on the Australian television show "Enough Rope" in 2003, he shared how he would often wake up "burning" with passion to get habitats for endangered species of wildlife around the world. He was using his wealth to buy up large tracts of land to make them wildlife reserves. His passion was so contagious that you could join him by becoming a "wildlife warrior". Tens of thousands did. Why? Because he turned his desire into a passion and he then positioned himself so it would become a REALITY.

I have discovered that the more we are mentored, the easier it is to see what our destiny looks like, and the easier it is to be released into it.

As T.D. Jakes says, "If you can see the invisible, you can do the impossible."

There is so much spoken and written about discovering your destiny. I've taught it for years too. However there is even a greater joy than helping sons and daughters discover what their God destiny is and helping them be established in it.

The truth is you can't stop with destiny discovery. Otherwise you are only a person who looks and never does.
We need inspiration.

As a young Christian I developed a habit of reading a new book each week. They were always inspirational stories of normal men and women doing amazing things for God. The inspiration was contagious. My spiritual life and passion exploded because of that habit. T.D. Jakes calls inspiration the "fuel" that ignites the PASSION. We need to overcome the inevitable obstacles that stand between our destiny and us now.

Coincidently, I also discovered that passion for God was very attractive to the opposite sex. Prior to becoming a Christian, girls certainly didn't flock to me. Suddenly all that changed. My wife still says that the main thing that attracted her to me was my passion for God! In my early Christian years I was so passionate for God that I wasn't that interested in relationships. Jesus had become my best mate as well as the lover of my soul and I wanted to tell everyone I could find. I still tell single young people that this is the best way to find your life destiny partner. The person of the opposite sex running beside you is often the best one to share your destiny quest. Sometimes all it takes is for God to open our eyes.

Inspiration is often in the form of an increasing burning inside of you. Two of the disciples experienced this on the road to Emmaus in Luke 24. Verse 32 says "Were not our hearts burning within us" as Jesus walked and explained scripture to them about his resurrection.

God will confirm the burning passion of your destiny many times over if you are looking and listening.

God will bring 'incidental fathering' across your path during the formative period of destiny development. As I began to be developed into my calling some remarkable things started to happen. Inspiration grows through divine confirmations. Twice in a three-month period after I stepped into ministry, I had dramatic inspiration events. The first was when I was one of 5000 people at a World Full Gospel Businessmen's Conference in Melbourne when I was twenty-eight years old. Reinhardt Bonnke was preaching during his first ever visit to Australia. The Holy Spirit was moving powerfully during the meeting. At one stage Reinhardt told all the audience to lay hands on person near you for the power of the Holy Spirit to fill each one for ministry. A lady seated behind me, who was from the USA and whom I had never met previously, leaned forward and began to prophetically declare that I was a "lion on God's battlefield of the Holy Spirit and I was filled with boldness to be used by Him." The second was in one of our own church services shortly after. During a greeting time, a visitor prophesied over me nearly the same word as the one I received in Melbourne.

Bobby Clinton, in his excellent book 'The Making of a Leader' calls these events *'ministry discovery confirmations.'* I know that each of these events powerfully shapes you for destiny fulfilment. He will do the same for you when you commit yourself to destiny fulfilment.

We need commitment

When you have commitment, T.D. Jakes says:-
- Inspiration moves to action

- Dates turn into wedding plans
- Good ideas are followed through on - and become business plans
- You formalize your commitment and start *doing* what you were created for
- You are prepared to sacrifice and do hard work to bring dream to REALITY

As a young Christian just out of college, the formalisation of my commitment took place when I decided to no longer follow the career path of an accountant. The passion for telling others about Jesus continued to grow in me. Often I would go witnessing in the main street of my hometown by myself. It didn't matter to me if the person was drunk or sober; they all had to know that Jesus would change their lives for good. All my friends and family knew that I had become a radical Christian. My father did not approve. But now I was more concerned what my Heavenly Father wanted for me! My radical commitment to 'the Jesus cause' would even unnerve my Christian friends. I just needed to be fathered in life. God sent a wise man of God to teach me how to balance passion with commitment to doing the things that would build my life into a son of God and eventually a spiritual dad.

If you don't have commitment, your life with be mundane. You will lose passion. It is at this point where trouble often begins as enthusiasm wavers. It starts very subtly. Recently I saw a married couple together at a coffee shop. One was reading the newspaper while the other sat there and there was no communication at all. What did that say about their relationship? They had lost their passion for each other. It can start very slowly but the result is that you also lose your commitment. The same will be true for every part of your life. You can go through the motions and do what is expected, but in the process you lose inspiration.

Be careful not to lose your dream

For most couples it is not about falling out of love but falling out of passion. What applies to marriages also applies to your destiny. We must keep passion alive. To do that means we must realign our focus. Perhaps you have to give your attention to this on a weekly basis. Death to destiny results if this is not addressed. This is very important but only the first step. To live your destiny YOU have to DO something!

Each of us must position ourselves for destiny. Recently I was asked to go to Africa on a mission trip by one of my spiritual fathers. I wouldn't have naturally gone on my own volition because I have a passion for the nations of the Pacific Rim, not Africa. Nevertheless I wanted to serve my apostolic fathers and the H.I.M. network, which was having its first conference in Kenya. It was the most amazing experience because many people were born again, healed and delivered. It was also the first ever H.I.M. apostolic network conference in Africa and it was so inspiring to see the bishops and pastors receive the message of apostolic reformation with enthusiasm. My life was changed dramatically as a result with a wonderful encounter with the Father heart of God. This would not have just happened - I still had to decide to go.

We earlier defined 'position' as the way in which a person is 'placed or arranged.' This is a powerful truth! For you to experience your destiny, you have to position yourself to experience it. Similarly for you to father spiritual sons and daughters you have to first position yourself as a son who is being systematically fathered!

It is the same for your blessing, healing, prosperity in fact any destiny desire. All those choices require faith and you must position yourself for fulfilment of that destiny. This may require great change or only a very minor adjustment. It will require change in your attitude and behaviour.

Favour comes when you position yourself for destiny...and so do obstacles

When we do step-up into destiny, our human nature sometimes takes over and we expect no problems. This is just not realistic. In 1997 our church went through a very painful time. A lot of people left due to lack of good leadership on my part. I had a choice at that time. I could see it as only a time of pain or I could see it as a destiny development moment. When we have times that we are disappointed, defeated or discouraged what do we do? We have a choice. We either go no further and give up or we keep going. It is never the time to stop. Instead it is your rise up time to experience your destiny. You need a Godly strategy to hold your course.

Keys to position you for Fathering a Destiny

First - Decide you will overcome all obstacles

I can guarantee that obstacles will come when you position yourself for destiny. It may be unexpected changes in your health, finances or even family. Don't be surprised, but be even more determined. When we first moved to live in the USA we had major car breakdown issues, my daughter had repeated trips to the doctor with asthma attacks, and even worse we had no permanent home for the first six months.

But Paul had the answer. It was focused determination. In Philippians 3:13 he said *"But this one thing I do, forgetting what is behind, I press on ..."* A classic example of this is found in Acts 3. Peter and John are on their way to the temple and go through the gate called Beautiful. There was a man sitting there begging who had been crippled from birth. He had been there forty years. Peter and John stopped and gave the man something much greater than what he had asked for. He was miraculously healed. Although something even more amazing happened. Acts 4 tells us that the result was that 5000 converted in one day. They also went to jail on that occasion as well (verse 17) because they were warned to stop and they wouldn't!

Then in Acts 5 they are back in jail again but this time their backs were whipped until they bled and were ordered not to speak in the name of Jesus anymore (verse 40).

I have a question for you. Did they stop despite these obstacles? The answer is no! (verse 41-42). The whole dynamic changed from threats to actual murder in Acts 6 and 7 but that did not change the way they responded.

We can see they did two important things in their determination to overcome all obstacles. We need to do the same 2 things!

1) Rise up in righteousness

Acts 6 tells of the story of Stephen. The apostles decided to choose seven men to wait on tables and daily distribute food to widows. The qualification was that they needed to be full of God's grace and power. They did miraculous signs and wonders among the people even though all hell broke loose through arguments and false accusations. But Stephen rose up in righteousness! Verse 10 says "they could not stand up against the wisdom of the spirit by whom he spoke". As they stoned him to death he spoke the most powerful response, "Lord, do not hold their sin against them". Regardless of the extreme opposition, righteousness shone through.

2) Look for God in the midst of obstacles

In Acts 8:1 all hell breaks loose but God didn't do the scattering and persecution. Satan did!! The Lord DID turn it around immediately for good. God will do the same for you. Joy Dawson calls this our 'reaction test' - that is when you have obeyed God and things go wrong. Joy says God tests our reaction when confronted with the enemy's plans. I call it "when life does not make sense" test. We all have a choice at that time. We can either respond in faith or trust God to stay the course or react in anger or panic, blame God and refuse to trust. If we do that we fail the test.

The answer is not to move out of our rise-up position but look to God in the midst of it.

In Jacob's case God turned persecution and death threats into destiny fulfilment. Jacob looked to God in the midst of obstacles (Genesis 32:26 - *"I will not let you go unless you bless me"*). We need to have the same determination as Jacob had.

All of us need to have this operating in our lives. We need to decide to overcome all obstacles.

Second - Expect that transformation will take place as you position yourself

Jacob indeed had favour and blessing over his life (see Genesis 30:43). Why? He expected God's favour to be over his life. He believed that he had honoured his father-in-law through hard work. Even though he was manipulated and exploited, he refused to become bitter. Instead he allowed these challenges to cause his destiny to get better. So God used a bad father to transform Jacob from a manipulator into a man of integrity and his destiny was transformed. This was the case even though Jacob's character was far from perfect. For that to happen he needed to take the risk faith step by returning home and facing the consequences of his past. We also need to take steps of faith toward our destiny that cause us to wrestle with our God cause!

Another powerful illustration of this fact is seen in the Apostle Philip's life. Philip saw amazing multiplication miracles and divine encounters. As a result he had incredible destiny fulfilment. Because he always stepped out boldly, he had supernatural experiences that changed lives and the lives of those people's descendants for generations to come. His Acts 8:26 encounter with the Ethiopian eunuch resulted in Ethiopia becoming the first Christian country in Africa from 316 AD. Because of Philip's obedience, the nation of Ethiopia has one of the largest Christian populations in Africa today. Destiny decisions always have supernatural impact for generations. That is why spiritual fathering is so important today. We have the opportunity to affect generations of people through our sons and daughters, long after we are gone. The favour of God always follows when you keep positioning yourself for destiny!

So fathering a person into their destiny has to be very intentional. The challenge for most leaders is that an older form of mentoring has been the only example we have had. As I shared in the Introduction, there has been confusion of understanding between discipleship, mentoring and fathering that has not helped. Most leaders would still refer to fathering as mentoring or discipleship. Apostolic fathering is a development from both. Mentoring typically requires those being mentored to "follow my example" (1 Corinthians 11:1) of the one doing the mentoring.

However I believe this Fathering Reformation emphasises three levels of mentoring – by those in front of us (we all need Apostolic

Alignment in the form of a spiritual father speaking into our lives); peer level support, accountability and encouragement (we can father our peers so it is not about age or title but function); and those younger than us in God.

This is intentional fathering of spiritual sons and daughters. It must be systematic. By that I mean it must be on a frequent basis in a formal setting so there can be continuity of input, accountability and reinforcing of 'new wineskin' thinking.

The most important distinction of apostolic fathering from the traditional concept of mentoring and discipleship is that it is 'next generational.' It involves the fathering of each person's unique destiny by a person who has a father's heart. Fathering is done intentionally and systematically. It builds, encourages, equips and then releases sons and daughters into their destiny to transform the lives of others and then reproduce themselves again and again in the generation following them!

Chapter 5

Fathering destiny attitudes

One of the first things that seem to happen when you enter a 'fathering relationship' is an adjustment in your attitude! Today's generation is full of attitude – but it is not the type of attitude that will build your life. In fact the reverse is the case. Most people don't see that their attitudes are destructive. Not only do those attitudes destroy relationships but they cause you to miss destiny opportunities when they come along. The problem is you were created for a divine purpose. If this is true, then you must develop a destiny attitude.

I was preaching at the large Bali Blessing Church in Denpasar, Indonesia in January 2008. Thousands of people were present! There was a phenomenal response to the altar call. What made it unique was the number of men that responded that night. I soon discovered that this was very unusual for that culture. The message given that night reinforced the destiny call of the church as a covenant people. It is my conviction that God puts each one of us in families. God also sets us in covenant church families. The senior pastor, Timothy Arafin, a wonderful father in God, later told me, "Kingdom people talk the same kingdom language when they have the same covenant destiny call." That was why so many Indonesian men responded that night. Even more important, people will position themselves for destiny when they understand how much our destiny blesses others and us.

God's desire is to bless us. Jeremiah 29:11 *"God has a plan to prosper you and give you a hope and a future."* Why? The answer is always 'covenant.' If you are a new believer, there is a new covenant between you and God because of Jesus. This new fathering reformation is re-establishing the power of covenant relationships through apostolic networks and alliances. God is drawing the hearts of spiritual fathers to sons and daughters and the hearts of the children to the fathers (Malachi 4:6) through covenant relationships.

Most Christians fail to realize the necessity to live in covenant with each other. Yet, the reality is, if they did they would experience significant development in their destiny!

We must not give just give mental agreement. We must begin to live out of the revelation that God is a covenant keeping God. God's COMMITMENT to humankind and RELATIONSHIP with us has always been on the basis of a COVENANT.

There are two important keys for our destiny.

First, you need to be in covenant with God for destiny fulfilment in your life. There are many covenants in the Bible. Each covenant in the Old Testament teaches us something specific. Noah's covenant with God in Genesis 6:17-19 tells us that God will establish covenant with us. In Genesis 15:18 and 17:1-7 we see Abraham's covenant contained both promises and conditions. Moses' covenant in Exodus 34:10-28 was conditional on the believer's obedience. When Jesus came, God's covenant with us changed dramatically. Matthew 26:27 tells us we are now subject to a new covenant that God has made with us through the blood of His son Jesus. It is a covenant of grace. It is not dependant on how good we are, as we can never be good enough. Covenant is a sacred treasure in the heart of God. God does not enter into them lightly and nor should we.

Second, you have to keep covenant with your spiritual family. It is very obvious to me that most Christians have no idea what covenant means. Covenant is "an unconditional commitment to an imperfect person". It means you don't walk away from those you are in covenant with, even when you are hurt or offended. You love no matter what. You cover each other's backs and always believe the best. It is one thing to join an apostolic network and say you are committed to the Apostolic Reformation, but you have to live it out through covenant relationship. This is dealt with in more detail in Chapter Seven - *"Fathering will save you from the destiny destroyers"*.

You have a responsibility in the outworking of that covenant both for your life and the fulfilment of the lives of those you influence.

The best way this works is by destiny actions. I have discovered the reason why Christians don't live their destiny is not the devil, or others, or circumstances, it is our wrong actions with wrong attitudes. The good news is, if someone has the wrong destiny attitude God will still work in their life.

The best example of wrong destiny attitudes is Moses' response to his destiny discovery. In Exodus 3 Moses experienced the 'burning' call of God on his life, one of the most obvious you could ever have. In verses 1-6 God appears to Moses supernaturally, *"Take off your shoes, you are on holy ground."* Those types of destiny encounters you never forget!

Even though it was not nearly as dramatic as Moses' call, in 1983, God was pouring out His Spirit powerfully in our church in Townsville. As well as many people being physically healed, restored and filled with the Holy Spirit, we had to keep moving walls and configuring our church building to accommodate the growing numbers. Then the Lord was very specific in His direction to us from Isaiah 54:3 *"Expand the place of your tent. Stretch your tent curtain wide."* It was a specific word to us at Praise Chapel from the written Word.

The elders and my senior pastor began a search for larger buildings. Eventually we decided we needed land to build a purpose built worship centre. As one of the team I was asked to help search for suitable parcels of land. After an extensive search we found three large areas of land that were suitable. Before a crucial board meeting when a decision was to be reached, I borrowed a trail motorbike and rode over all three areas. I spent time walking and praying over each one. When I got to the last block, even though we had been told the owner would never sell to us, as I prayed the Holy Spirit clearly said (as audible as I've ever heard God's voice.) "Take off your shoes and kneel down, you are standing on Holy ground". I obeyed and felt the Spirit's anointing coming on me very powerfully.

We quickly discovered that the block of land was for sale after all, so we bought twelve and half acres of land for $110,000 much to the amazement of real estate agents and housing developers. It was located on a major intersection, a road that would become a major access road for the northern highway into our city. What had happened? Destiny action had followed destiny attitude that God would build his church in the city regardless of what the real estate developers said.

That type of destiny encounter you never forget. God called Moses to be His voice to Pharaoh on behalf of the nation. Exodus 3:7 - *"I have indeed seen the misery of my people... and I am concerned about their suffering. So I have come down to rescue them."*

'Through you Moses, I'm sending you!' You can't get more specific destiny direction than that.

It was his destiny, his divine purpose, what a great day! Moses should have been thrilled, but he wasn't!

Sadly Moses didn't have a 'father figure' in his life at that time to help him. Instead he had the best excuses in the world.

Here are some principles that I've been taught to deal with. They are the five most used excuses that we all have made at some time or other.

Firstly, Moses said what so many of us think – '*Not me Lord, I'm not good enough.*' Moses used the best excuse first Exodus 3:11, "*Who am I...*". In other words he thought he was not qualified and not good enough. We can all feel this way but it is a wrong attitude! The truth is it is never about our goodness but God's goodness! We will never be good enough. This is why we need spiritual fathers. So at crucial times in the outworking of our call as sons and daughters, when self doubt comes, those who believe in us are there to guide us.

The issue is whether we are willing to be used by God. We have to come to the place where Jesus did in Luke 22:42 "*Not my will but yours be done.*" We must grow into that same attitude. This is how we learn to walk toward our destiny.

The second most used excuse by a lot of people is - '*What am I going to say?*'

It was the excuse that Moses used next. Exodus 3:13, "*...what shall I tell them?*"

If you think or speak like this then you are being insecure. You are focusing on your inadequacies not on who is inside you. But God says *"Don't worry... open your mouth and I will fill it."* Isaiah 51:16.

God said to Moses, *"Tell them "I AM has sent you' I will tell you what to say."* This is one of the hardest lessons to learn, as you have to overcome your own insecurity and rise up and be bold. Dr. David Yonggi Cho says, "We have enough Holy Spirit. We just need to be bold with what we have."

As a young leader, I would pray for hours before I would preach. One day the Lord told me that I had prayed enough and I needed to be bold and go and preach it in His strength! Something wonderful happens when boldness takes hold of you. You feel it rising on the inside of you. All the intimidation leaves. Sometimes I am even able to analyse what is happening when I am speaking and think 'where did I get those words from?' Jesus alluded to this type of experience when He said in Mark 13:11 *"...do not worry beforehand about what to say. Just say whatever is given you at the time, for it is not you speaking, but the Holy Spirit."*

The challenge is not to worry about what you are going to say. The more you learn to be spirit led, the more you will hear the voice of the Holy Spirit leading you. This is the key to growing as a son and daughter of Papa God (Romans 8:14). I now ask the Lord before I get up to speak "Daddy, what do you want to say tonight?" Without fail He will tell me what He wants to say and it always blesses the congregation. Why? As you learn to be an obedient son, He releases His blessing on you and through you. The great side benefit of doing this is that you no longer have to worry about what you are going to say! This doesn't mean you no longer prepare before you speak publicly. That is how immature children think. No. You are growing up as a son or a daughter and you prepare accordingly. Your Father does not want you to worry any more. It is not about the words. It is about the worry!

The third most used excuse - *'What if they don't listen to me?'*

This is the 'authority question.' It comes out of not knowing who you are in Jesus. The authority issue is imperative in our growth as spiritual sons and daughters of God. It is the key to our progress in growing up in God. This is dealt with more in Chapter Eight – "Growing your Father's heart to change this generation".

Sadly, we see in Exodus 4:1 that Moses' self-confidence (or lack of it) was only based on his own abilities. Your circumstances will never be subject to you and other people will never listen to you if you think this way.

Jesus response to our insecurities is always the same. It is not about you, it is about WHO is inside of you!

2 Corinthians 4:7 *"But we have this treasure in jars of clay to show this all surpassing power is from God and not from us."*

The real issue is not about you, but whether you will allow Him to flow through you.

To do this you have to be willing to get past your insecurities and look at His presence in you. You have Christ, the hope of glory inside you. Rise up in *His* strength and not your own.

Fourth excuse - *'I can't do it'*

When you are put in a difficult situation that is way out of our depth, the main thing to realize is you can't do it - but God can and will! Unfortunately if you only ever focus on the first part of this statement, negativity will grow in your attitude. This is what Moses allowed to happen to him. Exodus 4:10 says, *"I have never been able to speak properly."* The deterioration in attitude is nearly complete when you get to this stage. If you keep looking at your own strength you can't do it!

When we look to God and what He can do, He is then able to move with power in the most impossible situation! In Exodus 4:11 we see God's response to this 'I cannot do' attitude- *"who gave man his mouth?"* In other words, if God gave you a mouth and has placed you there for that purpose, then you can do it.

Jesus says just that about us! *"Everything is possible for them who believe..."* (Mark 9:23). Who is 'them'? US! We can do all things if we simply believe and believe simply!
I saved best (or worst) for last...

The Fifth excuse people use – *'It's too hard - send someone else'*

This is the ultimate negative mindset - and Moses had it!

Exodus 4:13, *"But he said, 'O my Lord, please send by the hand of whomever else you may send."* Look at God's response to this attitude in verse 14, *"the Lord's anger burned against Moses ..."* We need to understand that this attitude makes God angry!

Why? Because He has chosen us! If He's chosen us, then we can do it. Philippians 4:13 says, *"I can do all things through Christ who strengthens me."* So the 'too hard' attitude is a lie, it is not the truth!

If we only look with natural eyes you will only see things as too hard. Intimidation will always dominate your life and prevent you from stepping up into your destiny.

By now I hope you can see that these five attitudes will hinder you from experiencing your destiny. The answer is you need to change your attitude!

Change your attitude

We all need two types of attitude.

God attitude

The first attitude is a God attitude. What do I mean by a 'God attitude'? It is a *'desire to please God attitude'* and not yourself. It means that this is our motivation above everything else we do in life. David caught this very truth. He said in Psalm 37:4 *"Delight yourself in the Lord and He will give you the (destiny) desires of your heart."* The parenthesis is mine but it is a powerful revelation. If you put God first, destiny desires follow.

Psalm 145:19 confirms this, *".... He fulfils the desires of those who fear Him."* The word 'fulfils' is a destiny word. For your life to be truly fulfilled this is the only way to live. Sadly the reverse is also true as an ungodly attitude is destiny destructive.

We see that was the case with King Solomon in 1 Kings 11:1-11. God told him not to intermarry with other nations. Why? Destiny fulfilment for him and his nation was at stake. There was a covenant between God and Israel, but Solomon did not obey God! The result was Solomon's ungodly wives turned his heart to other gods (verse 4) so much so that he even worshipped them (verse 6.)

Here we have the wisest man who ever lived who no longer had 'Desire to please God attitude.' Instead, he had allowed ungodly desires in his life that were stealing his and his nation's destiny.

If it can happen to the wisest man, it can happen to us. Yes, even Christians today!

It is important to understand that we must make sure we have our attitude adjusted daily! The best way to do this is by intimacy with the Father. He speaks to us by the power of the Spirit when we spend time in His presence through the Word and worship. We are able to spend time listening to Him when we pray, rather than doing all the talking. This is the best way to keep a God attitude focus.

Good Attitude

The second type of attitude we need is a good attitude. The best example I have ever seen of a good attitude was by a church member in Townsville in the early 1980's named John (*Jungle* to his friends). His catch cry always was, "Praise the Lord mate!" One day his attitude faced the ultimate test. After pulling an engine out of an old church bus so he could remove and fix its gearbox, he spent hours putting it all back together only to find that he had missed fixing a crucial part of the gearbox! Did he have a bad attitude? Was he upset? Not at all! His catch cry was the only thing that rang out from under that bus! His good attitude redeemed a horrible and incredibly frustrating five hours as he repeated the entire task.

Esther had this attitude too! The thing I love about Esther is how good her attitude was even under incredible negative obstacles and pressure. When confronted with the need to speak up in the king's court at the threat of certain death, her attitude was "if I die, I die." Esther 4:16.

Paul tells us in Ephesians 4:23 that we are all able to 'put off' bad attitudes and 'put on' good attitudes because we are made new in the attitude of our minds.

The more we desire to have a God attitude we will have an attitude adjustment so that we will have a good attitude too!

Philippians 2:5 tells us that, *"Your attitude should be the same as Christ Jesus..."* So we must ask what Jesus' attitude was like. Primarily it was one of humility.

This seems to be the most common characteristic of destiny people! It is also the main characteristic that we observe in the apostolic fathers that God is raising up around the world. It is the thing that I love the most about my apostolic father Che` Ahn. For those who criticize this reformation as nothing more than self-appointed titles, they obviously don't understand this new wineskin. If you appoint yourself an apostle, then you are not one!

Our attitude must be the same as Christ Jesus. Paul tells us that in Philippians 3:3-5 to *"Do nothing out of selfish ambition or vain conceit, but in humility consider others better than yourselves. Each of you should look not only to your own interests, but also to the interests of others."*

Paul goes on to tell us that Jesus *"took on the nature of a servant"* and *"he humbled himself and became obedient to death."* (Philippians 3:7-8)

I have discovered that obedient people are spirit-controlled people. I love being around them, don't you? The greatest people I know are the most humble and most obedient. Those good attitudes are worth copying.

So we need an attitude of obedience as well as humility to have a good attitude.

For years I lived by the motto that 'Obedience = Blessing.' I have since discovered that a simple change was necessary to make it a destiny formula for all sons and daughters to follow as we grow a father's heart and as we father a destiny.

Humility (God attitude) + Obedience (Good attitude) = Destiny Fulfilment

People like Moses, Esther, Paul, Billy Graham, Heidi Baker, and Che` Ahn, all have it! And so must you if you want to experience your destiny and learn to grow into fathering the destinies of others.

Decide today to change your attitude to a God attitude and a good attitude and you will experience your destiny. Guaranteed!

Chapter 6

Learning to establish your destiny

One of the most important lessons to learn as an emerging spiritual father is that the development of your ministry is a process. Many times I have heard the Holy Spirit say "no life experience is wasted IF you are willing for me to build your life." The truth is that you have to learn to establish your destiny!

Ever since my good friend Lou Engle prayed for me two years ago, I have experienced what Lou calls the 'Dream Stream'. I dream spiritual dreams nearly every night. This is biblical of course. Acts 2:17 says, *"In the last days I will pour out my Spirit on all flesh and my young men will see visions and my old men will dream dreams."* I guess I come under the latter as I now dream all the time and they are not 'pizza' type dreams. God does seem to speak to me this way!

In one spiritual dream, I dreamt I was at a Christian rock concert. There was a sound check scheduled at five pm in which I had been asked to participate. I realised in the dream that I had a choice, either I could go along or I could stay at home. One thing was certain, the concert was happening regardless of my decision.

After I woke up, I reflected on the meaning of that dream. It was obvious to me that we cannot avoid our destiny in life! Even as you read this your destiny is taking place. Nonetheless we have a choice as to how our destiny is outworked in our lives. Time and time again, I have seen people miss their destiny opportunities because they lack the understanding that they need to make destiny decisions.

To establish your destiny there are two important things you must understand!

First you have to be able to clearly see and articulate the destiny of God for your life

Second you have to learn to live in the destiny process. This requires keeping a big picture perspective. That is why we need spiritual fathers who have a heart to see what is going on in our lives as part of the larger direction.
Fathers have to regularly ask the question, "How will that decision build your life and contribute to your destiny direction?" I am saddened when I see young emerging leaders who grab at any ministry promotion opportunity that comes along even if it means leaving their mentoring relationships and character formation process!

The truth is that you are all faced with destiny choices all the time. You choose everyday whether or not we have a mindset of faith when confronted with negative circumstances. You have a choice over your financial decisions, will you be either tied-up by debt or living free enough to obey God immediately when he tells you to go somewhere unexpected or give to someone you haven't thought of before. You have a choice with your employment. The choice should always be on the basis that you will fulfil your destiny. Our vocation can contribute or obstruct our destiny being established.

All these decisions require you to be obedient to God in your lives and not succumb to the pressure of your circumstances.

Fathers need to teach their sons the 'best choice principle.' This means that when you are weighing up the different options in major decisions, you must always ask what the best choice for you.

We were in that situation when we were living in the USA when my studies had stalled because I had to work full time to support my family. It seemed our dream to go home to Australia was looking more and more remote. It came to a head when my boss told me that he wanted to demote me but still give me the same workload. I knew I needed to change jobs but my best choice was to resign and go back to seminary full time, finish the remaining year and then go home to Australia to plant a church.

After much prayer and counsel from mentors we made the choice to do that at the end of year. It would mean that we would have no income for the next twelve months and live by faith. The day after our decision we were offered to be managers of our apartment complex, which reduced our rent substantially. I received a scholarship so all my college fees were paid for those twelve months. Then the first day of 1992, a complete stranger walked into our former church back in Australia with a gift for us of $5000. We lived off that money for six months. That same amount was given again in July. So by December 1992 my degree was finished and we were able to return home and we planted Set Free church a few months later. The best choice in this case was a destiny accelerator.

What happens when we don't make the best choice? They do have an effect of the progression of our destiny. Sadly, because of the lack of fathering or sons who are unwilling to heed wise advice, people often make choices that stall the establishment of their destiny. But as Jesse Duplantis says *"The great thing about dreams is that they never have an expiration date"*. God is good and when we return to him with a humble heart in obedience, he will make way for us to realign our lives back into our destiny.

If you visit The Rocks on Sydney Harbour, in Australia just left of where the ferries come in, there is a historic cottage that belonged to John Cadman. He is a great example of how destiny is a process. John was transported in 1798 to Australia as a convict for stealing a horse. But he did not allow this set back to put him off course in his destiny. He had a dream to be a free man, married and in charge of the government boats on the harbour. Despite the many obstacles, he did not give up. One day something exciting happened. He was released from jail and employed by the government as assistant government coxswain, after a conditional pardon was granted in 1814. He then received a free pardon in 1821. From January 1827 until December 1845 he was superintendent of government boats at Sydney and lived at a place of prominence on the harbour. When he retired in 1845, the Governor gave him a special commendation and spoke of 'his great respectability'. He ended his life as a significant historical figure in the formation of Sydney and is seen as an example of how this nation has become great!

One of the things that I teach my spiritual sons are that destiny does not need to be an abstract thing. It becomes very real when you make a decision to position yourselves for destiny. This means you have become destiny conscious and have chosen a destiny direction for your life. As a result all the life decisions you make should follow that destiny direction.

Some Christians wrongly believe that life will all just work out in the end! Like an elevator, regardless of the button pushed, ending up on the right floor. But this is not true! Destiny won't happen by itself. I believe that you need to be very specific about your life choices so you complement your life destiny.

Life is not like that, because that means there is no positioning involved. How many times have you heard someone interviewed and they said, "I just happened to be in the right place at the right time"? What they are really saying is, "I responded the right way when a destiny opportunity came my way."

If you don't believe this, let us examine a few 'what if' examples. What if Abraham, the father of many nations, had not obeyed God and stayed where he was living because he was too scared to just pack up and go without knowing where he was going? He would not have become the father of Israel and even worse Israel would not exist today as we know it.

What if Ruth had not made a covenant with Naomi & went home to her own country after her husband died? After all that would have been a reasonable decision. But she stayed because of a covenant destiny decision and met Boaz who became her new husband. Matthew 1:5 tells us that Boaz and Ruth had a son, Obed who was the father of Jesse, the father of David therefore it would be right to assume have that King David would have been born had not Ruth positioned herself for her destiny.

'What if' David had not fought Goliath because he was too afraid? He would have never been king. The reality is that the Book of

Psalms and Israel today would not exist as it is! Why? It was dependant on them to make correct destiny decisions. The ultimate 'what if' example is Jesus in the Garden of Gethsemane. What if Jesus had said, "It's too hard Father, I can't do it," or at the cross had summoned angels and killed his persecutors?

Then you and I would have no salvation, no forgiveness, and no love of God shed abroad in our heart. The end result would be no destiny fulfilment for any of us! Praise God that Jesus stepped up into His destiny!

The truth is generations are dependent on the choices you make today. Your future spiritual sons and daughter's destiny are dependent on the life decisions you make now.

As you read this I encourage you to stop and pray right now this prayer, *"Lord Jesus I ask you to show me your destiny for my life and help me to see it clearly. I decide to position myself for destiny today. I ask you for courage to make destiny decisions daily. I declare I will fulfil God destiny over my life in Jesus name."*

The second thing we need to do is to understand how our destiny grows

I have learnt that the way we expect our destiny to unfold isn't the way it always happens. In fact, it rarely happens the way we expect. This is what exactly happened to Joseph. In Genesis 37:4-10 we see that Joseph's Father loved him more than his brothers, they were envious of him. Joseph had destiny dreams where his brothers and father bowed down to him. Instead of this happening straight away, he went to prison instead. What a reality check!

When we learn to establish our destiny God does two things! He blesses us and establishes us even more. Destiny establishers happen when we keep doing the most important foundation acts in our lives. The most foundation acts involve learning to live in faith, hope and love (1 Corinthians 13:13). Heidi Baker asks the Lord at the end of each day 'Have I been kind to everyone I've met today?' What is she doing? She is teaching herself how to live in the foundation of love. The same principle applies to hope and faith too! Learning to live by faith is not hard but it does involve a change of mindset, a lot of obedience and a touch of risk! Same with living in hope – we must practise trusting God and others and believing in our destiny! With all three-foundation acts, the result is that fruit grows.

We have had family devotions every morning since the children were very young with great fruit in each of their lives. Lou Engle says that we must not have just one act of obedience, but a lifestyle of obedience. Acts 14:1 - *"At Iconium Paul and Barnabas went as usual into the Jewish synagogue"* not just once but daily. What were they doing? They were establishing their destiny.
It goes on to say, *"...they spoke so effectively that a great number of Jews and Gentiles believed."* Fruit always follows us building 'destiny establishers' into our lives.

We all love it when we are blessed by God! But God wants you to understand that blessing doesn't just happen by coincidence. You must modify your behaviour to establish it. These destiny establishing decisions involve a 'whatever it takes attitude'. The result of these choices is that God always blesses your life.

Before we were together, my wife Cheryl, in her first year of college, went through a time of being distracted in her relationship with God. But then she realized she couldn't live like that anymore because she knew she was going to marry a preacher. She had that strong sense of destiny ever since she was twelve years old when she encountered God on the steps of her home. She quickly realised that even though her destiny was strong over her life she needed to make lifestyle choices that would establish her accordingly.

How to establish your destiny

Make your destiny the centre of your mindset.

All successful people do this. The result is your mindset becomes so strong that it affects the way you see life. I have a Christian worldview. Everything I see in life is through that perspective. But it didn't just happen. I had to consciously change my mindset, values and way of living to make God's destiny the centre of my lifestyle and mindset. The best way to confirm your destiny is to step out and assess your mindset after the event. For example, if you have a sense that your destiny is to be used by God in the mission field then test the waters and go on a mission trip. You will soon know if this is your call or not!

It even affects our spending choices; if we are always buying things that won't help you achieve destiny goals. Your behaviour needs to be modified.

Exercise faith over your destiny

You must have faith that God did speak that destiny over you. Settle that now. No longer have any doubt over this! Either God's word is true or not. Jeremiah 29:11, *"For I know the plans I have for you,"* declares the Lord, *"plans to prosper you and not to harm you, plans to give you hope and a future"*. Only use faith words over your destiny. Remove all other words from the way you speak.

Modify your behaviour

Most people don't understand that if you don't modify your behaviour, your behaviour will modify your destiny in a negative way. How many times have we seen Christian girls marry non-Christians? Years later they are still struggling to be established in their destinies. Why? Their behaviour modified their destiny to such an extent that it took years for them to resurrect their destiny.

Decide to change any behaviour that steals from your destiny being established. This means you should only use faith actions for your destiny. Only do the things that will fulfil your destiny in the long run. It's important to start this now. Do you realise your career choices, friend choices and especially our relationship choices all shape our destiny now and in the future. Before I was a Christian, when I was sixteen years old, I was attracted to a girl down the street. I soon discovered the feeling was mutual. There was one problem was that whenever she spoke she swore constantly. Even though I wasn't saved I knew that this was not the girl for my future to be fulfilled so I chose to end the relationship.

This destiny behaviour modifying also includes you embracing the time delays and setbacks as part of establishing your destiny. Just look at what that did for Joseph, Moses and Paul. Joseph was proud and boasted about his destiny to his family. Moses had an anger issue that resulted in murder. Paul was an impatient man. He had little time for a young immature leader, John Mark, who had let him down previously. Yet later in his life he modified his thinking and said, *"Bring me John Mark for he is profitable to me"* (2 Timothy 4:11 KJV).

All of these people were able to modify their thinking and behaviour in line with their destiny because of the time delays they experienced. So if you have been frustrated that opportunities haven't been happening quickly enough for you, try embracing the time delays and ask God to show what behaviour needs to change to help establish your destiny.

What other things do you need to do to help establish your destiny?

Stop for a moment now and review your destiny choices. Have the courage to be honest and reconsider any choice that hasn't help establish your destiny.

Chapter 7

Avoiding the Destiny Stealers

One of the major lessons that all spiritual sons and daughters need to learn is what I call the 'the anomaly of the divine destiny'. Someone once described it as realising that our destiny is for 'now but not yet'. Time delays can be one of the major frustrations in an emerging leader's life. That goes for spiritual fathers and spiritual sons and daughters. When you first become aware of that destiny, it is so exhilarating to know that God wants to use you in a mighty way. You are so excited you tell everyone who will listen. You believe that it is going to happen and it is going to happen fast!

That is exactly what Joseph thought! And that is why he told his father and brothers his destiny dream about them and bowing down to him (Genesis 37:5-9).

It wasn't Joseph's dream that caused the problem. It was how he immaturely positioned himself by telling others who hated him. The result was an avalanche of events over the next thirteen years that sought to steal his God given destiny!

Even after you have discovered your destiny and have been established in it, you need to be still very much aware of what I call the 'destiny stealers'!

What are 'destiny stealers'? They are outside influences and events that will try to steal your focus from your destiny by distracting you. They can even be other people in your life including those close to you. Sometimes they can be well meaning Christians who project their inability to see God's plan in their own life onto you.

In Joseph's case, initially, it was his brothers. Even before Joseph had his dreams, there were problems. First of all though, Joseph was critical of his brothers to his father. Unwisely, his father loved Joseph more than the other sons. This is one of the worst examples of fathering I've seen. As a father of six children myself (five born, one adopted), I learnt very quickly that you cannot have favourites. All children must be treated the same. You need to be especially careful that you do this with your spiritual children too. There will always be one who will endear themselves to you the most but I have discovered that the answer is to spend an equal amount of time and interest with each of your children. Over the years I have had 'daddy dates' with each of mine growing up.

For apostolic fathering, a good solution for this issue is to regularly meet all together at the one time in a mentoring group so you equally father your spiritual sons. This means you have intentional fathering input on a regular basis. I have found that it must be done as regularly as weekly to systematically grow them and give them the accountability that they need. If you don't meet frequently, so many other things speak into the formation process that is happening inside them. You must intentionally become one of the consistent influences and in the process see remarkable growth and fruit.

Joseph's father, Jacob, did not do this. Even though he had long suffered at the hands of his own father-in-law, it is obvious that Jacob did not know how to father his sons the right way.

Genesis 37:4 tells us *"When his brothers saw that their father loved him more than any of them, they hated him and could not speak a kind word to him"*.

The sad reality was that his brothers hated Joseph so much that they wanted to kill him. Talk about getting your destiny stolen! The good news was that even when we do not know how to be a good Godly father, the father of all destinies, Abba Father, watches over us. God had a bigger plan for Joseph than satan's plan.

This is true for all of us. However, as we have learnt, God's destiny does not just happen. Our decisions and the decisions of others have a direct bearing on the timing and fulfilment of God's destiny for our lives and the lives of our spiritual sons and daughters. That is why I always tell my sons to take their time in getting their destiny decisions right. God is the god of the 'now' but he is never is in a hurry when it comes to Christ being built and formed in us! So there is no need to rush destiny decisions. We have always maintained that you never make a destiny decision (like marriage, career change, buying or selling a house, leaving your church family to go to another city) when you are excited, emotional, sick, tired, stressed, financially stretched or discouraged. Sadly, there are numerous instances over the years, where good people have 'rushed in where angels fear to tread'.

The good news is that even when we mess up, God is still with us! When we keep our heart right with God, He still watches over our destiny. Even in the midst of the heartache of poor choices or discrimination by others, God will still make a way.

This was definitely the case in Joseph's life. Instead of killing him, God used his brother Rueben to convince the rest of his brothers to sell Joseph into slavery. Even then God was with Joseph. It expresses itself through the favour of God.

Genesis 39:2-3 tells us that *"The LORD was with Joseph and he prospered, and he lived in the house of his Egyptian master. When his master saw that the LORD was with him and that the LORD gave him success in everything he did."*

Joseph also had to face other destiny stealers. This time it was not his doing but the wife of Potiphar, his master. Joseph was unjustly accused of attempting to molest his master's wife and thrown into prison.

Again this did not result in Joseph's destiny being stolen. There was more distractions and delays but God's favour was still working to his good.

Destiny stealers are more than irritating they are dangerous.

They might often only appear minor but their effect is still significant. Distractions can come in the form of financial pressure, sickness, relationships or work trouble. They can rise up as strife as happened in Acts 14:2. Here the Jews who refused to believe and stirred up trouble against Paul and Barnabas. Sadly, this is fairly frequent in church life where people forget they are in covenant with each other.

Destiny stealers also result from major events that happen to you. Maybe you have experienced a relationship breakdown or have been sacked from a dream job, or even been persecuted for your faith. Worse still it might involve the death of a family member. All of these events can derail you from your focus on your divine purpose if you allow those events to steal your destiny through discouragement. Too often Christians blame God for these problems but it is not God's doing. It is always the work of satan the enemy of our souls.

In February 2008, there was an attempted coup by rebels against the government of East Timor, which included an assassination attempt on the President José Ramos-Horta. He was on his morning walk when he heard gunfire and saw smoke coming from the direction of his home. He was even advised by a passer-by that rebels had invaded his home and killed some of his staff. He easily could have hidden or escaped. Instead he chose to go home to protect his family and staff. As he approached his home he was shot and critically injured. After being flown to Australia for medical treatment, he spent months in rehabilitation. As soon as he was strong enough, he subsequently returned to East Timor to continue his leadership. He refused to allow this attempt on his life to stop him and steal his destiny to lead his nation.

Sadly some destiny stealers are from the most unexpected sources. Often through people we love and trust.

In 2 Samuel 15, David's own son, Absalom, plotted to overthrow his father's kingdom. Absalom stood at the city gate for four years trying to undermine his father's authority.

Verse 6 says, *"Absalom behaved in this way towards all the Israelites who came to the King asking for justice, and so he stole the hearts of the men of Israel."*

Initially David was weak and did nothing. It appeared that Absalom was able to steal David's destiny and become king (2 Samuel 15-17). We see how David had to flee in fear for his life. It appeared that his destiny to be Israel's greatest king had been stolen from him.

But in 2 Samuel 19, we see where David had to make a destiny decision. He had a choice to make. Either to mourn and give-up or to reign and stand for his destiny! David had to deal with the destiny stealer once and for all. Verse 8 says *"So the king got up and took his seat (place) in the gateway."* The very place where Absalom stood for four years, David sat down.

His destiny action spoke very clearly that he would not allow anyone to steal his destiny- even his own son! The act of sitting down was a kingly act of him exercising his authority. 2 Samuel 19:14 says that David won back the hearts of all the men of Judah. There comes a time for each of us when we stand-up in our destiny position, just like David did.

Destiny stealers always come from outside. They often seem to be 'good' ideas but they are never 'God' ideas. They can even be the influence of other Christians. We need to learn to recognise them for what they are! They are destiny stealers. We must learn to become ruthless in removing them from our destiny focus.

How do we deal with destiny stealers?

Rejoice

Philippians 4 says we must learn to rejoice - even in the most difficult and hopeless situation. We must do what verse 4 tells us to do in the midst of our heartache. Rejoicing is a posture of faith. And it is act of warfare. That is why it is so important. Rejoicing also restores our soul.

We need to change our perception purposely

Joseph was able to do this successfully twice, both as a servant and as a prisoner. He made sure he did not become resentful or bitter because of his circumstances. We must be sure we live like this 'in the midst of' overcoming the destiny stealers. Always ask yourself the question – 'What does His Word say about this to me?' I've also learnt how to deconstruct the assignment of the enemy. You need understand the power of 'binding and loosing' that Jesus taught His disciples in Matthew 18:18 *"Truly I tell you, whatever you bind on earth will be bound in heaven, and whatever you loose on earth will be loosed in heaven."*

Most Christians have never been taught how to pull apart piece by piece that enemies assignment sent to steal your destiny. Try it.

To do this we must have a paradigm shift to God's perspective on the destiny stealers. Then we must discipline ourselves to only think this way.

We have to practice living a lifestyle of destiny

We need to do it daily. As Philippians 4:9 says, *"Whatever you have learned, or received or heard from me, or seen in me - put it into practice."* It is important to put these antidotes into practice. One of the best ways to do this is to be accountable to a mentor or a spiritual father on a consistent and regular basis.

The question is, how do we respond when these destiny stealers happen? The answer is to be determined to progress in your destiny.

Chapter 8

Fathering will save you from the Destiny Destroyers

One of the saddest things is when you see someone with great potential make choices that destroy their career, marriage and even destiny.

In May 2006, Wendell Sailor, a famous dual international rugby football player, was tested positive for cocaine. One of the most successful, popular, and flamboyant rugby players had his million dollar contract torn up and was banned from playing professional sport for two years. What happened? Wendell's actions caused his career to come crashing down. His destiny was being destroyed by his life choices.

As well as things from outside us coming to steal our destiny, there is also another force at work – the Destiny Destroyers!

One of the saddest things is to see a great life crumble because of these destiny destroyers!

What are they?

Where do they come from?

Destiny destroyers come from within us. They are where our actions and/or decisions cause us to walk away from our destiny altogether.

Wendell Sailor was able to turn his career around after the two years suspension and is now back on track because he listened to a father figure in his life – Wayne Bennett. Wayne Bennett's coaching success is legendary because he fathers his young men on how to live life responsibly as well as his ability to inspire young me who to win championships. Wendell went to his former coach and asked for help. Fathering saved his career. One of the things Wendell had to do was to take responsibility for his actions and deal with the destiny destroyers in his life.

We are responsible for identifying these destiny destroyers in our lives and dealing with them. No one else! Recognise them for what they are. Don't make excuses or call them mistakes. Tell the truth to yourself and to others.

If we don't, marriages will fail, friendships end, careers are lost and families are broken. Many think because that they are Christians that their destiny will just happen as they go through life and they are immune from destiny destroyers. This is just not true!

I've often said the main reason why a church or ministry will grow is the Christian leader. The same leader is the main reason why it doesn't grow! I am sure you know of high profile leaders whose ministries suddenly disintegrated. The truth is the cracks in the foundations of their personality or character were always there but they didn't deal with these foundational issues. Largely it was because of the lack of fathering & accountability.

Paul says in 1 Corinthians 4:14-16 *"I am not writing this to shame you, but to warn you, as my dear children. Even though you have ten thousand guardians in Christ, you do not have many fathers, for in Christ Jesus I became your father through the gospel. Therefore I urge you to imitate me."*

A New Wineskin

There is a "fathering reformation" going on in the body of Christ right now! It is not a re-emphasis of something old.

It is a new wineskin – a new way of doing church and life. It is what I call 'apostolic maturity' as opposed to 'apostolic ministry.' So it is not so much resurgence in the teaching on the five-fold spiritual functions of Ephesians 4, but a discovery of the need to complement the development of spiritual authority with character and maturity. The best way to do that is to grow up from being a son to a mature father!

The supernatural should be evident in every true apostle except in this Apostolic Reformation, God is as interested in maturity in your life as much as the manifestation of signs and wonders. This is important for developing for the destiny of God for every person. Christlike character is especially essential in a true father.

One of the dilemmas in the church has been the moral failures of famous Christian leaders. The question asked is –"How can they manifest the miraculous and yet be unrighteous in areas of their life?"

Prophet Bill Hamon in his book 'Apostles, Prophets and the Coming Move of God' speaks of just this. *"Just because a person can manifest the supernatural in prophetic and apostolic ministry does not guarantee that his or her doctrine is right or their personal life is Christlike.....Never be swayed to believe that a man's teaching and revelations are correct because he can manifest the miraculous"* (p36).

There are so many so-called 'apostles' and 'prophets' who badly need to be fathered today! It is sad to see a person in ministry who is struggling because they have become too famous too quickly. As a result, they tend not to listen to those around them. Che Ahn's most frequent comment concerning these situations is "that person needs a spiritual father." Sonship will always be the best foundation of strong fathering. The keys are two-fold - learning to be a son of God and learning to listen to a spiritual father.

Because God is 'no respecter of persons' He will bless the life of imperfect people who seek to serve Him. He does that for you and He does that for me! When convergence starts to come in a person's ministry these character flaws begin to show up under the spotlight if they have not been dealt with! They will come up the more fame and the more your character comes under pressure. If there is not mentoring and accountability – what I call Apostolic Fathering of these men and women of God, then the 'destiny destroyers' have their free reign!

There are four common 'destiny destroyers.'

1. DOUBT

The first destiny destroyer is doubt.

Doubt is very familiar to us because it is the original destiny destroyer. Adam and Eve in Genesis 3 doubted that God really did say not to eat of the tree of the knowledge of good and evil. Doubt is also the number one temptation.

Even Jesus in Luke 4:9 was challenged to doubt who He was! *The devil led him to Jerusalem and had him stand on the highest point of the temple. "IF you are the Son of God............"*

In the first Adam, doubt stole his destiny. The second Adam, Jesus, did not give in to the temptation to doubt.

When Jesus tells the Parable of the Sower in Mark 4 there is a secondary meaning to this parable. It is not just the Word of God that is stolen out of people's hearts! We see in verse 15 that satan takes the 'word' or destiny out of those hearts too. This is what doubt does. It steals from our destiny.

The truth is, you just can't tell your destiny to everybody, because often they will doubt you. Why? The answer is that it is too big for them to grasp because it's not their dream, but yours. So sometimes, even if you have dealt with doubt, the unwholeness of others can cause you to doubt your destiny! That is the time to separate you from all the doubters! Choose to only associate with men and women of faith who dare to dream and believe God for the impossible. You need a spiritual father who believes in you and your destiny.

Don't allow doubt to dominate your circumstances or your mind. Instead be ruthless with doubt. Kick doubt out! Refuse to allow doubt to destroy your destiny!

2. OFFENCE

The second most prevalent destiny destroyer is offence. Once doubt destroys God's Word from the heart, the next stage is always offence.

This is also the next stage in the Parable of the Sower.

Mark 4:16-17 *"...like seed sown on rocky places, hear the word and at once receive it with joy. ¹⁷But since they have no root, they last only a short time. When trouble or persecution comes because of the word, they quickly fall away."*

It could also read - *"The seed is sown on stony ground and because it has no root...it endures for a time but when affliction or persecution arises for the word's sake immediately they are OFFENDED".*

Offence steals destiny out of your heart and Christians are exceedingly good at it!

One of the saddest things that often happens when a person's destiny is delayed, is that it often results in them getting angry and offended at God. For years I could not understand why people do this as I have always seen God as a good God. Only good things come from Him. Largely, their own choices have put them in that predicament. Yet God gets the blame when things don't work out. Then I realised that people who get mad at God do so because they don't know His father's heart. They don't truly know God as a father because their own natural relationship with their earthly father has been so painful. Don't get mad with God. Get offended at offence. Hate it as an enemy. Do all that you can to come in the opposite spirit! Ask God to show you where that offence entered and ask the Holy Spirit to heal that part of your personality so you are free.

Jesse Duplantis tells the story of going to minister in a church in the USA and the pastor had a special offering to honour him. After he had finished ministering, the pastor informed him the offering had not covered the expenses and they could not give him anything! Jessie said that this was equivalent to them stealing the offering. The natural tendency would have been not to go back there again! However he decided to keep accepting their future invitations for the sake of the people and to ensure that offence had no place in his heart.

Offence is insidious. It creeps up and enters your heart even when you are not consciously aware of it being there. The key to overcoming offence is to keep short accounts of forgiveness and to walk in love.

3. THE FLESH

The third most powerful destiny destroyer is the cares of the world or what the bible calls 'the flesh'. This causes the most immediate loss of destiny.

Nothing undermines your authority, your anointing and eventually your destiny more quickly than a fully developed fleshly character flaw.

Mark 4:18-19 talks about how the cares of the world choke the word of destiny in our hearts. We have a choice when confronted with temptation, to sin or not. Adultery and fornication are the more obvious examples of this. Over and over again I hear of well-known preachers succumbing to this destiny destroyer. Sadly because the marriage covenant is also broken, many others are hurt and even have their destinies stolen from too! A pastor who chose this road has taken ten years of pain to try to recover his marriage. Sadly, just recently, he has finally given up all hope of restoring that which was once powerful and beautiful. It was because of one act of flesh in 1998.

Another well known evangelist in Australia in the 1980's had struggled with homosexual temptation for many years. Even though he was married and had children, he finally left his wife and moved in with his male lover. Years later, we ran into each other. He was so bitter about life and especially his brothers and sisters in Christ. Yet it was always his choice. Had he chosen to get help and walk in weekly accountability with transparency with an Apostolic Father he would be still be married today and living in his destiny!

Flesh not dealt with will always destroy your destiny! The answer always is to take the lid off and let the light of Christ in by confessing your sin or temptation to another! James is right when he says *"Confess your sins one to each other and pray for each other so that you may be (will be) healed"* (James 5:16)

When you are fathered it means you are able to be transparent and accountable in every area of your life – especially with temptations of the flesh. Actively pursue mentoring relationships that will give you this level of accountability.

Maturity is not about how well we function in ministry (preach, lead, minister in the anointing, pursuing our calling) but how we PROGRESS in our GROWING UP!

4. DISCOURAGEMENT

The largest number of people destinies is destroyed when they give up because of discouragement.

Howard Hendricks from the Navigators once said that the number one weapon Satan will use against a Christian is discouragement. He calls it the "leukaemia of the soul".

They become so discouraged that they stop pursuing their destiny. Jonah came to that place. Even after surviving a 'whale of a time' he got discouraged at God's compassion to Nineveh (Jonah 4). He became angry at God and wanted to die (verses 8-9).

You have a choice when discouragement comes. Either give up or stand firm!

The one thing I have learnt is that when you reach out to your spiritual father during these times they will help you to see your circumstances from a different perspective. This is the power of this Apostolic Fathering. You don't have to feel alone. The person who believes in you will speak into your life just at the right time. That is how God, our Heavenly Father, arranges it.

Eventually it is up to you to encourage yourself with God's promises and to live continuously in intimacy with Him. If you do that the discouragement will not stay. It leaves.

Another way to say it is to paraphrase 1Timothy 6:1 - *"Resist the 'destiny destroyers' and they will flee from you."*

We see this over and over in the early church. A great example is in Acts 14:3 where Paul and Barnabas despite great opposition, *"spent considerable time there speaking boldly for the Lord."* In other words, they would not stop regardless of how discouraging the persecution and opposition were! They refused to stop and give up their destiny, even when all hell broke loose (see verses 5-7).

Be determined to pursue fathering relationships. Do not allow these relationships in your life to deteriorate. Discouragement causes you to give up your God destiny and be even more determined not to allow poor integrity actions to destroy your destiny.

If you don't have a fathering relationship, ask God for one.

As you adopt an apostolic fathering mindset, He will start to bring others around you who are also on this journey. This is how Apostolic networks function. He will start connecting you supernaturally with those who are emerging spiritual fathers who understand this new wineskin revelation. Before long you will have a supernatural relationship with someone who is willing to walk in a fathering relationship with you. This is called "Apostolic Alignment" which is discussed in the next chapter.

Chapter 9

Growing your Father's heart to change this generation

How do you grow a father's heart?

By becoming the spiritual father or mother that you were created to be! This involves a commitment to do whatever it takes in your life to grow our sonship into fatherhood. Once you get the revelation from heaven that this is 'why you exist', then you start to develop in that identity and authority. The result is that you WILL become a father to the next generation.

Fathers know who they are. They know their identity and not just their role in life!

Our true identity grows out of intimacy with Father God.

This is how we become the adopted son or daughter of God. This is who we are and what we were created for. Out of that identity comes authority to change circumstances and lives here on earth. This is how God's kingdom comes on earth through us!

To become a spiritual father you have to intimately know God as a Father. Even though I have been on a journey of intimacy, the problem for most men in western culture is that we have been a part of a fatherless generation. Like so many others, my natural father had problems expressing affection and as a result like most adult males (and many females) in our culture, I have never truly heard my father expressing his love to me. I never had a problem loving Jesus or getting to know the voice of the Holy Spirit within me. However having a deep loving intimate relationship with God my Father seemed far removed because of my experience with my earthly father.

Something happened recently to change all that. I was at Heidi Baker's Iris Ministries in Mozambique in July 2009. It is Heidi's custom to ask all the visitors to come forward for prayer during her Sunday service. What is unique about this is that she gets the children from their orphanage to lay hands on you and pray for each visitor. My encounter with these children was life changing. They don't pray short cute prayers for a few minutes. They prayed intense prayers of love and passion for me that lasted thirty minutes. I have never had anyone pray for me for that long before, let alone two children.

After twenty minutes my heart was so moved that I began to weep and weep. I realized that I was the one that was fatherless. I had the orphan spirit while the orphans had been adopted (by Heidi and God the Father). This broke my heart even more. Then something else happened. As they kept praying, I saw a scroll float down from heaven to me. The top of it read 'Certificate of Adoption' and my name was on it! I finally realized that my Papa Daddy God had adopted me. I had 'known' it intellectually for over thirty years but this was the first time that it resulted in true intimacy with God. I had a change of identity. I had moved from being an orphan to a son!

Things have changed since then for me. Why? My identity changed when I had a revelation of the father heart of God that my Father wanted to form in me.

God wants us to know His father's heart so He can grow a father's heart in us!

The first thing we have to do is to turn our heart to him. Malachi 4:6 *"He will turn the hearts of the fathers to their children, and the hearts of the children to their fathers......"*

When we first take a step to soften our heart, He turns His father's heart toward us.

Jesus taught us that in what is known as the parable of the prodigal son. For me the power of this parable is how the father responded when he saw his son coming home even though he was still a long way off. Luke 15:20 tells us that his father was filled with compassion for his son and he ran to him. God the Creator and Ruler of the universe, the King of all kings, runs to us with compassion and love and declares, *"this son of mine was dead and is alive again"* (verse 24). It is time to come alive to the heart of the Father.

David as a boy learned how to worship God while he was out minding the sheep. His worship grew out of his intimacy with God. He was so anointed that evil spirits left when he played for King Saul (1 Samuel 16). So it is not a surprise that many years later when he had become king he would write in Ps 143:5-6 *"I remember the days of long ago; I meditate on all your works and consider what your hands have done. I spread out my hands to you; my soul thirsts for you like a parched land."*

Intimacy begins when our heart is turned toward Him in worship. So much so that we soften our opinions, judgements and mindsets and focus on Him.

Intimacy with God is so important. Out of it flows our sonship – the manifestation of the father heart of God to us and the planting of the heart of a father in us!

Romans 8:14-16 tells us that those who are led by the Spirit of God become sons of God and that spirit of sonship results in a deep intimacy with God as our Abba Father, Papa Daddy.

Recently in one of our revival meetings the male worship leader led us to a wonderful place of intimacy with God. Although when he started to sing "I kiss you with the kisses of my mouth" and "You have one arm under my head and one arm under my waist" I started to freak out. I couldn't relate and I told God that I was having trouble worshipping Him that way. I was struggling with the Aussie male macho thing. You know we can't get too intimate!! Or can we? I felt God prompt me with the thought " What if you were a three year old boy and your daddy picked you up and put one arm under your head, the other under your waist and hugged you against his chest. Could you relate to that then?" Something deep in my soul emphatically said "Yes!" It is time for men to get over the intimate obstacle and drop our guards and let the love of the Father into our heart for relationship.

How long does it take to get intimate with God? It only takes a revelation that you can know God intimately now.

The word "intimate" does not appear in the bible. The term *know* does. To *know God* is not an intellectual knowing. That is what is based on information only and breeds religion. To "know" someone in the bible means to be very intimate. So intimate in fact that the word "know' is used to describe sexual intimacy between a husband and wife. In John 21:15-19 Jesus, after His resurrection, has his famous encounter with Peter on the beach when he asked *"Simon, son of Peter, do you truly love me?"* three times. Each reply Peter said "Lord, You know I love you!" But Jesus was asking Peter, *"Peter do you **know** me intimately?"* Peter was answering "I love you as a friend". That was not the answer Jesus needed. I believe Peter twice used the word "know" to mean an "intellectual knowledge" but the third time he said "you know I know you intimately". It was only at that point Jesus felt Peter was ready to lead His church.

Out of intimacy, comes identity!

At Jesus' baptism, the Holy Spirit came upon Him with power. Most people stop reading there but something else happened. All who were present heard an audible voice. Matthew 3:17 – *"This is my son whom I love; with Him I am well pleased."* Prior to this statement there is no recorded supernatural ministry of Jesus.

Kevin Dedmon in his book 'The Ultimate Treasure Hunt' tells us that two things happened that day. Jesus was empowered by the Holy Spirit and his authority increased dramatically.

Why? It was because of his identity as the Son of God!
We need to know WHO we are. But our identity comes from being a Son of God. This is the greatest thing we can ever be known as – a Son of God!

Out of our identity comes our authority.

The centurion in Matthew 8 knew what authority was. To him it was seamless. There was no argument or options or possibility that healing would not take place. He told Jesus "..... just say the word and my servant will be healed." Even though Jesus called that 'great faith' it seems to me that there was also a great understanding of authority present. Why? The centurion knew who he was and how authority worked through him. We are able to have the same confidence in our authority because our identity has been found in Him.

Bill Johnson teaches that having a revelation of our true identity determines the level of kingdom authority we walk in and the amount of influence we have in bringing God's kingdom to earth.

Our intimacy with our Father God gives us so much identity that we can step out in authority representing Him. When we really know who we are, we can speak and act with great boldness. This was demonstrated very powerfully when Jesus was confronted by the reality of Lazarus' death in John 11, and declared to Martha in verse 3 *"Your brother will rise again"*. What was Jesus doing? Because He knew who He was, He was exercising the authority that was His. He used that authority to declare that Lazarus would be raised from the dead. Martha could not comprehend this and reacted with a religious response. Just like Martha, it is my observation that many Christians often criticize the spiritual experiences of others, out of their lack of understanding.

Lance Wallnou says that those who experienced the last move of God typically criticize and even persecute the next move of God. Religion is the greatest obstacle to this Fathering Reformation because it has all the clever answers but no power!

Religion is sterile. It does not reproduce spiritual sons and daughters. We have a generation of impotent believers who once had the potential to be fathers and mothers of God. They justify their inability to reproduce and their sterility by criticising the emerging generation of sons and daughters instead of fathering them! That is what religion does. It removes the power to reproduce. Rail against religion in you - it will kill the reproductive life in you! You will lose the spirit-led lifestyle

Martha had the personification of the power and authority of God standing before her, but did not recognise Him. So much so that Jesus had to say *"I am the **resurrection** and the **life**. He who believes in me will live, even though he dies"*. Jesus then put His words into action. Lazarus became the manifestation of that resurrection power and came back to life when Jesus exercised His kingdom authority here on earth!

Jesus understood how to reflect the heart of the Father as a Son! He was totally dependent on the Father so much that we are told that *"the Son can do nothing by himself; he can do only what he sees his Father doing, because whatever the Father does the Son also does"* - John 5:19. This is the key to keep on growing the Father's identity and authority in us. The more we do what we see the Father doing, the more we will reflect our Father's heart to others. I've found that our motivation will change greatly. It will no longer be self centred. It will be so much 'Father centred' that it will be reproduced in our sons and daughters. Our sons and daughters will do as we do by becoming fathers and mothers themselves. Then they will reproduce themselves over and over again. This is how people groups grow and this is how the kingdom of God grows – through reproduction! This is how an awakening in our nation will truly take place.

Through a Fathering Reformation!

The great news is that we too can bring God's kingdom authority here and now, when we walk in our true identity as fathers of sons and daughters of God. This is the result when we truly reflect the father heart of God and the fulfilment of our destiny now!

The best way to progress your destiny is by growing a father's heart in you.

In the process you will find your destiny being established as you grow in foundation acts of formation and character. I am convinced that we must continually resist the 'destiny stealers' and fight to reverse the 'destiny destroyers' by the strategic and consistent lifestyle of fathering relationships.

The result is that your destiny will begin to be fulfilled in you and through you to the spiritual sons and daughters that God will bring to you.

Make a decision today to live in destiny progression by growing as a son into a father.

This next generation is waiting and desperately needing to be fathered by you!

ENDNOTES

Chapter 2

1. Che Ahn – "Apostolic Alignment, Accountability and Spiritual Authority" – Harvest Rock Church, Pasadena, CA - 14th April 2008

2. John W McElroy - "Passing on the Baton"
Publisher: Arrow Publications www.stormharvest.com.au

3. Shampa Rice - www.irisministries.com/ministry-home.cfm?location=**india**

Chapter 3

1. T.D. Jakes – "Reposition Yourself" - Living life without limits
Publisher: Atria Books

Chapter 4

1. T.D. Jakes – "Reposition Yourself" - Living life without limits
Publisher: Atria Books P 47-51

Chapter 8

1. Dr. Howard Hendricks – Navigators – www.resources4discipleship.com/speakers

Chapter 9

1. Kevin Dedmon – "The Ultimate Treasure Hunt" A Guide to Supernatural Evangelism through Supernatural Encounters
Publisher: Destiny Image www.destinyimage.com

To contact the author, arrange speaking engagements or additional resources:

Bruce Lindley

Email – admin@arcglobal.org

www.arcglobal.org

www.ingramcontent.com/pod-product-compliance
Lightning Source LLC
Chambersburg PA
CBHW050439010526
44118CB00013B/1599